69- 10345

JAN 26 '72

APR 2 0 '70

THE NARRATIVE OF
WILLIAM W. BROWN
A FUGITIVE SLAVE

AND A LECTURE DELIVERED BEFORE THE
FEMALE ANTI-SLAVERY SOCIETY OF SALEM, 1847

THE NARRATIVE OF
WILLIAM W. BROWN
A FUGITIVE SLAVE

AND A LECTURE DELIVERED BEFORE THE
FEMALE ANTI-SLAVERY SOCIETY OF SALEM, 1847

With an introduction by

LARRY GARA
Wilmington College

ADDISON-WESLEY PUBLISHING COMPANY
Reading, Massachusetts
Menlo Park, California · London · Don Mills, Ontario

Addison-Wesley's
FUGITIVE SLAVE NARRATIVES

CONTENTS

INTRODUCTION

"It is a terrible picture of slavery," commented Edmund Quincy about William Wells Brown's newly written manuscript, "told with great simplicity. . . . There is no attempt at fine writing, but only a minute account of scenes and things he saw and suffered, told with a good deal of skill, propriety and delicacy." Quincy was an abolitionist editor and the son of Harvard's president. When Brown asked him to read the manuscript, he intended only to glance at a few pages, but found it so good he could not put it down until interrupted by a call to dinner. He readily agreed to write a letter to be prefixed to the book, and suggested to the author only "one or two alterations and additions."[*]

Brown's narrative quickly became a best seller and took its place with the memoirs of Frederick Douglass, Moses Roper and other former slaves whose writings contributed to the growing antislavery sentiment in the northern states. Whatever their literary merits, the works of ex-slaves had the ring of authenticity. Unlike the white abolitionists, these men could not be accused of speaking without knowledge and experience of the South's "peculiar institution." A contemporary writer said of the slave narratives that they were "calculated to exert a very wide influence on public opinion" because they contained "the *victim's* account of the workings of this great institution."[†] An abolitionist editor saw in them an "infallible means of abolitionizing" the North. "Argument provokes argument,"

---

[*]Edmund Quincy to Caroline Weston, July 2, 1847 in the Weston Papers, Boston Public Library.

[†]Ephraim Peabody, "Narratives of Fugitive Slaves," in the *Christian Examiner,* 47:64 (July, 1849).

he said, "reason is met by sophistry; but narratives of slaves go right to the hearts of men."*

For William Wells Brown, born a slave in Kentucky around 1816, publication of his memoir brought fame and probably some monetary compensation. The first edition of a thousand hardbound and two thousand paperbound copies cost him less than eleven cents a copy, and it was quickly out of print.† Within two years he sold out four editions totalling eight thousand copies.‡ With its personal approach and vivid pictures of slave life, Brown's narrative quickly found a receptive audience. In addition to the American versions, it was translated into several foreign languages and circulated in European editions. The book was only the first of a notable series of literary productions from Brown's pen. In 1848 he published a short anthology of antislavery songs, *The Anti-Slavery Harp,* and in 1852 his travel book, *Three Years in Europe,* appeared in London and Edinburgh. The following year he published a novel, *Clotel, or the President's Daughter,* whose main character was an alleged mulatto child of Thomas Jefferson. Though it could not compete successfully with *Uncle Tom's Cabin,* it was the first novel published by an American Negro, and as such was a significant work. Brown wrote several dramas about slave life and published one in 1848: *The Escape; or, a Leap for Freedom.* In *The Black Man, His Antecedents, His Genius, and His Achievements* Brown traced Negro history back to its African origins and included short biographical sketches of notable colored persons. Other writings included *The Negro in the Rebellion,* and several historical volumes expanding on the material first presented in *The Black Man.* The number of his publications is impressive and contemporary critics were nearly unanimous in praising their quality.

It is the second, or 1848, edition of Brown's memoir which is reprinted in this volume. He made very few changes from the first edition, but he added several appendices and this new edition contains as well a transcript of a speech he made in November, 1847

---

*Quoted in Charles H. Nichols, "Who Read the Slave Narratives?," *Phylon,* 22:153 (1959).

†Samuel May, Jr. to Dr. John Bishop Estlin, January 13, 1848 in the May Papers, Boston Public Library.

‡Peabody, "Narratives," 64.

to the Female Anti-Slavery Society of Salem, Massachusetts. The narrative was written thirteen years after Brown's escape from slavery and reflects, therefore, both the conditioning of his long contact with abolitionists and the vagaries of detail implicit in writing from distant memory. Nevertheless, it is full of insights about slavery and the ante bellum South which only a former slave could know. Furthermore it is important both because of the impact it had on thousands of readers and because of the wealth of material it contains.*

Even before publishing his narrative William Wells Brown was known as an effective antislavery speaker, one of a number of former slaves whose message reached many northerners untouched by the white abolitionist crusader.[†] In his talks Brown emphasized the terrible injustice of slavery as an institution which deprived individuals of their humanity, and he also included impressive eye-witness accounts of the cruelties which were sometimes practiced in the South. His lectures were well written and eloquently delivered, and he often drew large audiences both in America and in Great Britain, where he sometimes appeared in company with William and Ellen Craft, a famous fugitive slave couple from Georgia. Brown's lectures were occasionally illustrated with his own panorama of slavery, and after he wrote his antislavery plays he often substituted a dramatic reading for the usual lecture. In 1857 William Lloyd Garrison attended one of Brown's readings in Philadelphia and he reported it was "well delivered and well received" though the audience on that occasion was disappointingly small.[‡] A Vermont reporter commented that Brown held an audience breathless for nearly two hours with his wit and speaking ability. "His dignity of manner, his propriety of expression were more than we had expected to see in one who had spent the early part of his life as a slave," he

---

*Some of the basic factual material of Brown's life remains obscure, and the details differ in the several editions of his memoirs. At various times, for instance, Brown gave three different birthdates and also varying versions of his parental background. In one account Brown claimed that his mother was Daniel Boone's daughter.

[†]Larry Gara, "The Professional Fugitive in the Abolition Movement," *Wisconsin Magazine of History,* 48:196-204 (Spring, 1965).

[‡]William Lloyd Garrison to his wife, May 18, 1857 in the Garrison Papers, Boston Public Library.

commented.* A New York reporter found one of Brown's dramas, "in itself, a masterly refutation of all apologies for slavery, and it abounds in wit, satire, philosophy, arguments and facts. . . ."† Although early in Brown's career antagonistic mobs sometimes interrupted his meetings, for the most part he was greeted with enthusiasm. He continued to give lectures on Negro history after the Civil War ended slavery. In 1868 the *New York Evening Post* described one of his historical lectures as "intensely interesting" and an "able and manly vindication of his race from the charge of natural inferiority."‡

Unlike Frederick Douglass, his more famous contemporary, Brown never broke with William Lloyd Garrison and the moral suasion school of abolitionists, though their reactions to him and his contribution varied considerably. "It is a long time since I have seen a man, white or black, that I have cottoned to so much as Brown, on so short an acquaintance," said Edmund Quincy. Brown, he said, was an "extraordinary fellow," with "no meanness, littleness, no envy or suspiciousness about him."§ An English abolitionist reported to Garrison that a whispering campaign regarding Brown's personal life involving an alleged love affair was wholly without foundation and that he was a "sensible, excellent fellow." ‖ On the other hand some of the abolitionists were suspicious of the former slave's motives. Samuel May, Jr., when he learned of Brown's impending trip to England, noted that he was "a very good fellow, of very fair abilities and has been quite true to the cause. But he likes to make popular and taking speeches, and keeps a careful eye upon his own benefit." Brown owed everything to the Garrisonian cause, said May, "and he ought to be true to it." As it turned out, Brown consistently defended the Garrisonians during his stay in England.

---

* New York *Anti-Slavery Standard*, October 20, 1855.

† William Wells Brown, *The Escape; or, A Leap for Freedom. A Drama in Five Acts,* Boston, 1858, p. 52.

‡ Printed circular advertising Brown's lecture on the "Origin and Early History of the African Race," to be delivered in Boston's Tremont Temple, May 10, 1858, in the Garrison Papers.

§ Edmund Quincy to Caroline Weston, July 2, 1847 in the Weston Papers, Boston Public Library.

‖ John Bishop Estlin to Garrison, June 7, 1852 in the Garrison Papers.

Still the Garrisonians were concerned that certain of Brown's actions would hurt the cause. When his marriage seemed in danger, they urged reconciliation with his wife.* When Brown undertook to buy his freedom, they were further troubled. In 1847 Brown sent a copy of the first edition of his memoir to Enoch Price, his former master, who wrote Edmund Quincy expressing a willingness to free Brown for three hundred and twenty-five dollars. To the Garrisonians it was a matter of principle not to pay a slaveholder anything to manumit a person who was already free by natural and divine right. Brown agreed and wrote his former master that he could not accept the offer. "God made me as free as he did Enoch Price," he wrote, "and Mr. Price shall never receive a dollar from me or my friends with my consent."† Nevertheless, English friends, worried about Brown's safety under the new Fugitive Slave Law, apparently persuaded him to allow the transaction, for on July 7, 1854 it was completed for three hundred dollars.‡ While some of the American abolitionists were able to sympathize with Brown's dilemma and eventual decision, others were appalled. Sarah Pugh, a Philadelphia Quaker, asked an Irish friend if Brown had consented to be bought. "I hope he has not," she added, "for he would lose half his manhood."§

Despite the misgivings of his antislavery friends, William Wells Brown suffered no loss of manhood or of courage as a result of his manumission. Indeed, it gave him a new sense of security which freed him to continue his labors for antislavery and other reform causes. For in addition to abolition, Brown actively supported the peace crusade and the temperance movement. It was partly to participate in an International Peace Congress in Paris that he first traveled to Europe in 1849. He spoke at the meeting but found little support for

---

*Samuel May, Jr. to John Bishop Estlin, May 21, 1849 in the May Papers, Boston Public Library; Amy Post to Wendell Phillips, June 20, 1850, and William Wells Brown to Garrison, September 15, 1848 in the Garrison Papers. Brown was never reconciled with his wife, who died while he was in Europe. He later remarried.

† Quoted in William Farmer's "Memoir of William Wells Brown," in Brown, *Three Years in Europe,* London and Edinburgh, 1852, p. xxi.

‡Josephine Brown, *Biography of an American Bondman by his Daughter,* Boston, 1856, pp. 96-98.

§Sarah Pugh to Richard Webb, May 22, 1854, in the Garrison Papers.

his introducing antislavery matters into the proceedings, and left the Congress disillusioned with its results.* He gave longer service to the cause of temperance, organizing a temperance society among the colored population of Buffalo during his nine-year stay there. After the Civil War Brown joined several temperance groups and in 1871 at the Boston meeting of the National Division of the Sons of Temperance of North America he presented strong arguments in favor of admitting the colored delegates from Maryland to its deliberations. He also helped organize and became president of the National Association for the Spread of Temperance and Night Schools among the Freed People of the South.†

For William Wells Brown, however, the plight of America's colored people, whether slaves or nominally free, was always uppermost. The unique contribution of the fugitive slave speakers was to personalize slavery and remove its operations from the realm of abstract ideas. But for Brown and the others the battle against slavery was only half the war—the other was the battle against prejudice and discrimination in the North as well as in the South. In his books and in the letters he wrote to newspapers Brown called attention to the indignities suffered by colored people in the free states. A letter from England recalled the discrimination he had encountered on steamers, in hotels, in coaches, railways, and even in churches where he was forced to sit in a "Negro pew." When he arrived in Britain, he said, for the first time in his life he felt truly free.‡ In his first travel book he wrote, "our country is the most despotic in the wide world, and to expose and hold it up to the scorn and contempt of other nations, is the duty of every coloured man who would be true to himself and his race."§

Prejudice, he believed, was clearly a corollary of slavery. "One of the bitterest fruits of slavery in our land," he wrote, "is the cruel spirit of caste . . . ." It was a most foolish prejudice, without a

*W. Edward Farrison, "William Wells Brown," *Phylon,* 9:16 (First Quarter, 1948).

†William Wells Brown, *The Rising Son; or, The Antecedents and Advancement of the Colored Race,* Boston, 1874, p. 25.

‡"Memoir of William Wells Brown" in Brown's *Clotel; or, The President's Daughter,* London, 1853, p.41.

§William Farmer, "Memoir of William Wells Brown," in Brown's *Three Years in Europe,* p. 311.

"single logical reason to offer in its defence." Black people were mistreated in America only because "of their identity with a race that has long worn the chains of slavery." Black in itself was not bad. Brown pointed out that black clothing was often preferred to either white or colors, that black eyes and black hair in women often attracted men, and that men and women dyed their hair black, only to "curse the negro for a complexion that is not stolen."*

Brown was determined that all Americans should recognize the falsity of the doctrine of the natural inferiority of colored people. In his study *The Black Man* he met and refuted this misrepresentation, calling attention to the early black civilizations of Ethiopia and Egypt, as well as to many colored Americans "who, by their own genius, capacity, and intellectual development," surmounted the obstacles created by slavery and prejudice and "raised themselves to positions of honor and influence." Benjamin Banneker he described as a man of African parents whose blood was never corrupted "by a drop of Anglo-Saxon." Nat Turner, like Napoleon, "regarded himself as a being of destiny." He compared Toussaint L'Ouverture with George Washington, and said Samuel R. Ward was "never ashamed of his complexion, but rather appeared to be proud of it." Brown's list of Negro notables included poets, preachers, rebel slave leaders, painters, educators, actors, lawyers, and rulers of Haiti and Liberia. It was an impressive volume and, though some of his sources and conclusions would not pass the test of modern scholarship, he made his point and in the process he revived a virtually forgotten Negro past. Negroes, he said, should be proud of their heroes whose achievements proved the doctrine of inferiority a lie. "All I demand for the black man," he asserted, "is that the white people shall take their heels off his neck, and let him have a chance to rise by his own efforts."†

To the Negroes, Brown preached a mixed gospel of self-respect, hard work and self-improvement. In his last book, *My Southern*

---

*William Wells Brown, *The Negro in the American Rebellion: His Heroism and His Fidelity*, Boston, 1867, pp. 39, 361-362.

†William Wells Brown, *The Black Man, His Antecedents, His Genius, and His Achievements*, New York and Boston, 1863, pp. 5-6, 51, 59, 285, 49.

Home, published in 1880, he viewed slavery in a more benevolent light than he ever had before. The postwar plight of the colored people of the South he blamed on their religion and mode of living. There was an entire disregard of the laws of physiology, a tendency towards extravagant dress and an almost total lack of organized efforts to improve their lot. "Those who do not appreciate their own people will not be appreciated by other people," he declared. The black people must take up their own struggle for elevation, exhibit pluck and use all available spare time, day and night, to educate themselves. He advised Negroes to emigrate from the South as a first, necessary step in their improvement, and above all, he admonished, "black men, don't be ashamed to show your colors, and to own them."*

William Wells Brown took his goal of full equality from the American dream stemming back to the Declaration of Independence, yet much that he wrote foreshadowed some of the ideas of twentieth century Black Nationalism. His passionate resentment of all forms of discrimination and his repeated insistence on the need for colored people to cultivate self-respect and dignity on their own terms are clearly an aspect of current thinking. Yet only a few scholars have recognized his many contributions.† Saunders Redding, the noted Negro writer, described Brown as the first Negro novelist, playwright and historian whose list of accomplishments "argues his place."‡ Nevertheless, Brown's name remains unknown to many who are familiar with the writings and achievements of his contemporary, Frederick Douglass. When he died in Chelsea, Massachusetts in 1884 he was buried in an unmarked grave.

An unusually effective reformer, writer of history, fiction and drama, and an individual whose own life was an irrefutable argument agains racial inferiority, William Wells Brown deserves a better fate

---

*William Wells Brown, *My Southern Home: or, The South and Its People,* Boston, 1880, pp. 188, 237, 253.

†For many years Professor W. Edward Farrison of the English Department of North Carolina College has been collecting material for a Brown biography and publishing articles on aspects of Brown's career.

‡Quoted by Arna Bontemps in "The Negro Contribution to American Letters," in John P. Davis, Ed., *The American Negro Reference Book,* Englewood, N. J., 1966, p. 869.

than history has accorded him. Hopefully, the publication of his narrative and one of his antislavery talks will stimulate a new interest in this remarkable man and his many contributions to the American heritage.

Wilmington, Ohio   L.G.
October 1967

NARRATIVE

OF

WILLIAM W. BROWN

A

FUGITIVE SLAVE

WRITTEN BY HIMSELF

———— Is there not some chosen curse,
Some hidden thunder in the stores of heaven,
Red with uncommon wrath, to blast the man
Who gains his fortune from the blood of souls?

Cowper

SECOND EDITION, ENLARGED

BOSTON:
PUBLISHED AT THE ANTI-SLAVERY OFFICE,
No. 21 Cornhill
1848

NOTE TO THE SECOND EDITION

The first edition, of three thousand copies, of this little work was sold in less than six months from the time of its publication. Encouraged by the rapid sale of the first, and by a demand for a second, edition, the author has been led to enlarge the work by the addition of matter which, he thinks, will add materially to its value.

And if it shall be instrumental in helping to undo the heavy burdens, and letting the oppressed go free, he will have accomplished the great desire of his heart in publishing this work.

LETTER

From

EDMUND QUINCY, ESQ.

Dedham, July 1, 1847.

To William W. Brown

My Dear Friend:—I heartily thank you for the privilege of reading the manuscript of your Narrative. I have read it with deep interest and strong emotion. I am much mistaken if it be not greatly successful and eminently useful. It presents a different phase of the infernal slave-system from that portrayed in the admirable story of Mr. Douglass,* and gives us a glimpse of its hideous cruelties in other portions of its domain.

Your opportunities of observing the workings of this accursed system have been singularly great. Your experiences in the Field, in the House, and especially on the River in the service of the slave-trader, Walker, have been such as few individuals have had;—no one, certainly, who has been competent to describe them. What I have admired, and marvelled at, in your Narrative, is the simplicity and calmness with which you describe scenes and actions which might well "move the very stones to rise and mutiny" against the National Institution which makes them possible.

You will perceive that I have made very sparing use of your flattering permission to alter what you had written. To correct a few errors, which appeared to be merely clerical ones, committed in the

---

*Narrative of the Life of Frederick Douglass, an American Slave, Written by Himself (Boston, 1845).

hurry of composition under unfavorable circumstances, and to suggest a few curtailments, is all that I have ventured to do. I should be a bold man, as well as a vain one, if I should attempt to improve your descriptions of what you have seen and suffered. Some of the scenes are not unworthy of De Foe himself.

I trust and believe that your Narrative will have a wide circulation. I am sure it deserves it. At least, a man must be differently constituted from me, who can rise from the perusal of your Narrative without feeling that he understands slavery better, and hates it worse, than he ever did before.

I am, very faithfully and respectfully,

Your friend,

EDMUND QUINCY

PREFACE

The friends of freedom may well congratulate each other on the appearance of the following Narrative. It adds another volume to the rapidly increasing anti-slavery literature of the age. It has been remarked by a close observer of human nature, "Let me make the songs of a nation, and I care not who makes its laws;" and it may with equal truth be said, that, among a reading people like our own, their books will at least give character to their laws. It is an influence which goes forth noiselessly upon its mission, but fails not to find its way to many a warm heart, to kindle on the altar thereof the fires of freedom, which will one day break forth in a living flame to consume oppression.

This little book is a voice from the prison-house, unfolding the deeds of darkness which are there perpetrated. Our cause has received efficient aid from this source. The names of those who have come from thence, and battled manfully for the right, need not to be recorded here. The works of some of them are an enduring monument of praise, and their perpetual record shall be found in the grateful hearts of the redeemed bondman.

Few persons have had greater facilities for becoming acquainted with slavery, in all its horrible aspects, than WILLIAM W. BROWN. He has been behind the curtain. He has visited its secret chambers. Its iron has entered his own soul. The dearest ties of nature have been riven in his own person. A mother has been cruelly scourged before his own eyes. A father—alas! slaves have no father. A brother has been made the subject of its tender mercies. A sister has been given up to the irresponsible control of the pale-faced oppressor. This nation looks on approvingly. The American Union sanctions the deed. The constitution shields the criminals. American religion sanctifies the crime. But the tide is turning. Already, a mighty under-current is sweeping onward. The voice of warning, of remonstrance, of rebuke, of entreaty, has gone forth. Hand is linked in hand, and heart mingles with heart, in this great work of the slave's deliverance.

The convulsive throes of the monster, even now, give evidence of deep wounds.

The writer of this Narrative was hired by his master to a *"soul-driver,"* and has witnessed all the horrors of the traffic, from the buying up of human cattle in the slave-breeding states, which produced a constant scene of separating the victims from all those whom they loved, to their final sale in the southern market, to be worked up in seven years, or given over to minister to the lust of southern *Christians.*

Many harrowing scenes are graphically portrayed; and yet with that simplicity and ingenuousness which carries with it a conviction of the truthfulness of the picture.

This book will do much to unmask those who have "clothed themselves in the livery of the court of heaven" to cover up the enormity of their deeds.

During the past three years, the author has devoted his entire energies to the anti-slavery cause. Laboring under all the disabilities and disadvantages growing out of his education in slavery—subjected, as he had been from his birth, to all the wrongs and deprivations incident to his condition—he yet went forth, impelled to the work by a love of liberty—stimulated by the remembrance of his own sufferings—urged on by the consideration that a mother, brothers, and sister, were still grinding in the prison-house of bondage, in common with three millions of our Father's children—sustained by an unfaltering faith in the omnipotence of truth and the final triumph of justice—to plead the cause of the slave; and by the eloquence of earnestness carried conviction to many minds, and enlisted the sympathy and secured the cooperation of many to the cause.

His labors have been chiefly confined to Western New York, where he has secured many warm friends, by his untiring zeal, persevering energy, continued fidelity, and universal kindness.

Reader, are you an Abolitionist? What have you done for the slave? What are you doing in his behalf? What do you purpose to do?

There is a great work before us! Who will be an idler now? This is the great humanitary movement of the age, swallowing up, for the time being, all other questions, comparatively speaking. The course of human events, in obedience to the unchangeable laws of our being, is fast hastening the final crisis, and

> "Have ye chosen, O my people, on whose party ye shall stand,
> Ere the Doom from its worn sandal shakes the dust against our land?"

Are you a Christian? This is the carrying out of practical Christianity; and there is no other. Christianity is *practical* in its very nature and essence. It is a life, springing out of a soul imbued with its spirit. Are you a friend of the missionary cause? This is the greatest missionary enterprise of the day. Three millions of *Christian*, law-manufactured heathen are longing for the glad tidings of the gospel of freedom. Are you a friend of the Bible? Come, then, and help us to restore to these millions, whose eyes have been bored out by slavery, their sight, that they may see to read the Bible. Do you love God whom you have not seen? Then manifest that love, by restoring to your brother whom you have seen his rightful inheritance, of which he has been so long and so cruelly deprived.

It is not for a single generation alone, numbering three millions—sublime as would be that effort—that we are working. It is for Humanity, the wide world over, not only now, but for all coming time, and all future generations:—

> "For he who settles Freedom's principles,
> Writes the death-warrant of all tyranny."

It is a vast work—a glorious enterprise—worthy the unswerving devotion of the entire life-time of the great and the good.

Slaveholding and slaveholders must be rendered disreputable and odious. They must be stripped of their respectability and Christian reputation. They must be treated as "MEN-STEALERS—guilty of the highest kind of theft, and sinners of the first rank." Their more guilty accomplices in the persons of *northern apologists,* both in Church and State, must be placed in the same category. Honest men must be made to look upon their crimes with the same abhorrence and loathing with which they regard the less guilty robber and assassin, until

> "The common damned shun their society,
> And look upon themselves as fiends less foul."

When a just estimate is placed upon the crime of slave-holding, the work will have been accomplished, and the glorious day ushered in—

"When man nor woman in all our wide domain,
Shall buy, or sell, or hold, or be a slave."

J. C. HATHAWAY

Farmington, N. Y., 1847.

NARRATIVE

CHAPTER 1

I was born in Lexington, Ky. The man who stole me as soon as I was born, recorded the births of all the infants which he claimed to be born his property, in a book which he kept for that purpose. My mother's name was Elizabeth. She had seven children, viz.: Solomon, Leander, Benjamin, Joseph, Millford, Elizabeth, and myself. No two of us were children of the same father. My father's name, as I learned from my mother, was George Higgins. He was a white man, a relative of my master, and connected with some of the first families in Kentucky.

My master owned about forty slaves, twenty-five of whom were field hands. He removed from Kentucky to Missouri when I was quite young, and settled thirty or forty miles above St. Charles, on the Missouri, where, in addition to his practice as a physician, he carried on milling, merchandizing and farming. He had a large farm, the principal productions of which were tobacco and hemp. The slave cabins were situated on the back part of the farm, with the house of the overseer, whose name was Grove Cook, in their midst. He had the entire charge of the farm, and having no family, was allowed a woman to keep house for him, whose business it was to deal out the provisions for the hands.

A woman was also kept at the quarters to do the cooking for the field hands, who were summoned to their unrequited toil every morning at four o'clock, by the ringing of a bell, hung on a post near the house of the overseer. They were allowed half an hour to eat their breakfast, and get to the field. At half past four a horn was blown by the overseer, which was his signal to commence work; and every one that was not on the spot at the time, had to receive ten lashes from the negro-whip, with which the overseer always went armed. The handle was about three feet long, with the butt-end filled with lead, and the lash, six or seven feet in length, made of cow-hide, with platted wire on the end of it. This whip was put in requisition very frequently and freely, and a small offence on the part of a slave furnished an occasion for its use. During the time that Mr. Cook was overseer, I was a house servant—a situation preferable to that of a field hand, as I was better fed, better clothed, and not obliged to rise at the ringing of the bell, but about half an hour after. I have often laid and heard the crack of the whip, and the screams of the slave. My mother was a field hand, and one morning was ten or fifteen minutes behind the others in getting into the field. As soon as she reached the spot where they were at work, the overseer commenced whipping her. She cried, "Oh! pray—Oh! pray—Oh! pray"—these are generally the words of slaves, when imploring mercy at the hands of their oppressors. I heard her voice, and knew it, and jumped out of my bunk, and went to the door. Though the field was some distance from the house, I could hear every crack of the whip, and every groan and cry of my poor mother. I remained at the door, not daring to venture any further. The cold chills ran over me, and I wept aloud. After giving her ten lashes, the sound of the whip ceased, and I returned to my bed, and found no consolation but in my tears. Experience has taught me that nothing can be more heart-rending than for one to see a dear and beloved mother or sister tortured, and to hear their cries, and not be able to render them assistance. But such is the position which an American slave occupies.

My master, being a politician, soon found those who were ready to put him into office, for the favors he could render them; and a few years after his arrival in Missouri he was elected to a seat in the legislature. In his absence from home everything was left in charge of Mr. Cook, the overseer, and he soon became more tyrannical and cruel. Among the slaves on the plantation was one by the name of Randall. He was a man about six feet high, and well-proportioned, and known as a man of great strength and power. He was considered the most valuable and able-bodied slave on the plantation; but no matter how good or useful a slave may be, he seldom escapes the lash. But it was not so with Randall. He had been on the plantation since my earliest recollection, and I had never known of his being flogged. No thanks were due to the master or overseer for this. I have often heard him declare that no white man should ever whip him—that he would die first.

Cook, from the time that he came upon the plantation, had frequently declared that he could and would flog any nigger that was put into the field to work under him. My master had repeatedly told him not to attempt to whip Randall, but he was determined to try it. As soon as he was left sole dictator, he thought the time had come to put his threats into execution. He soon began to find fault with Randall, and threatened to whip him if he did not do better. One day he gave him a very hard task—more than he could possibly do; and at night, the task not being performed, he told Randall that he should remember him the next morning. On the following morning, after the hands had taken breakfast, Cook called out to Randall, and told him that he intended to whip him, and ordered him to cross his hands and be tied. Randall asked why he wished to whip him. He answered, because he had not finished his task the day before. Randall said that the task was too great, or he should have done it. Cook said it made no difference—he should whip him. Randall stood silent for a moment, and then said, "Mr. Cook, I have always tried to please you since you have been on the plantation, and I find you are determined not to be satisfied with my work, let me do as well as I may. No man has laid hands on me, to whip me, for the last ten years, and I have long since come to the conclusion not to be whipped by any man living." Cook, finding by Randall's determined look and gestures, that he would resist, called three of the hands from their work, and commanded them to seize Randall, and tie him. The hands stood still;—they knew Randall—and they also knew him to be a powerful man, and were afraid to grapple with him. As soon as Cook had ordered the men to seize him, Randall turned to them, and said—"Boys, you all know me; you know that I can handle any three of you, and the man that lays hands on me shall die. This white man can't whip me himself, and therefore he has called you to help him." The overseer was unable to prevail upon them to seize and secure Randall, and finally ordered them all to go to their work together.

Nothing was said to Randall by the overseer for more than a week. One morning, however, while the hands were at work in the field, he came into it, accompanied by three friends of his, Thompson, Woodbridge and Jones. They came up to where Randall was at work, and Cook ordered him to leave his work, and go with them to the barn. He refused to go; whereupon he was attacked by the overseer and his companions, when he turned upon them, and laid them, one after another, prostrate on the ground. Woodbridge drew out his pistol, and fired at him, and brought him to the ground by a pistol ball. The others rushed upon him with their clubs, and beat him over the head and face, until they succeeded in tying him. He was then taken to the barn, and tied to a beam. Cook gave him over one hundred lashes with a heavy cowhide, had him washed with salt and water, and left him tied during the day. The next day he was untied, and taken to a blacksmith's shop, and had a ball and chain attached to his leg. He was compelled to labor in the field, and perform the same amount of work that the other hands did. When his master returned home, he was much pleased to find that Randall had been subdued in his absence.

CHAPTER II

Soon afterwards, my master removed to the city of St. Louis, and purchased a farm four miles from there, which he placed under the charge of an overseer by the name of Friend Haskell. He was a regular Yankee from New England. The Yankees are noted for making the most cruel overseers.

My mother was hired out in the city, and I was also hired out there to Major Freeland, who kept a public house. He was formerly from Virginia, and was a horse-racer, cock-fighter, gambler, and withal an inveterate drunkard. There were ten or twelve servants in the house, and when he was present, it was cut and slash—knock down and drag out. In his fits of anger, he would take up a chair, and throw it at a servant; and in his more rational moments, when he wished to chastise one, he would tie them up in the smoke-house, and whip them; after which, he would cause a fire to be made of tobacco stems, and smoke them. This he called *"Virginia play."*

I complained to my master of the treatment which I received from Major Freeland; but it made no difference. He cared nothing about it, so long as he received the money for my labor. After living with Major Freeland five or six months, I ran away, and went into the woods back of the city; and when night came on, I made my way to my master's farm, but was afraid to be seen, knowing that if Mr. Haskell, the overseer, should discover me, I should be again carried back to Major Freeland; so I kept in the woods. One day, while in the woods, I heard the barking and howling of dogs, and in a short time they came so near that I knew them to be the bloodhounds of Major Benjamin O'Fallon. He kept five or six, to hunt runaway slaves with.

As soon as I was convinced that it was them, I knew there was no chance of escape. I took refuge in the top of a tree, and the hounds were soon at its base, and there remained until the hunters came up in a half or three quarters of an hour afterwards. There were two men with the dogs, who, as soon as they came up, ordered me to descend. I came down, was tied, and taken to St. Louis jail. Major Freeland soon made his appearance, and took me out, and ordered me to follow him, which I did. After we returned home, I was tied up in the smoke-house, and was very severely whipped. After the major had flogged me to his satisfaction, he sent out his son Robert, a young man eighteen or twenty years of age, to see that I was well smoked. He made a fire of tobacco stems, which soon set me to coughing and sneezing. This, Robert told me, was the way his father used to do to his slaves in Virginia. After giving me what they conceived to be a decent smoking, I was untied and again set to work.

Robert Freeland was a "chip of the old block." Though quite young, it was not unfrequently that he came home in a state of intoxication. He is now, I believe, a popular commander of a steamboat on the Mississippi river. Major Freeland soon after failed in business, and I was put on board the steamboat Missouri, which plied between St. Louis and Galena. The commander of the boat was William B. Culver. I remained on her during the sailing season, which was the most pleasant time for me that I had ever experienced. At the close of navigation I was hired to Mr. John Colburn, keeper of the Missouri Hotel. He was from one of the free states; but a more inveterate hater of the negro I do not believe ever walked God's green earth. This hotel was at that time one of the largest in the city, and there were employed in it twenty or thirty servants, mostly slaves.

Mr. Colburn was very abusive, not only to the servants, but to his wife also, who was an excellent woman, and one from whom I never knew a servant to receive a harsh word; but never did I know a kind one to a servant from her husband. Among the slaves employed in the hotel was one by the name of Aaron, who belonged to Mr. John F. Darby, a lawyer. Aaron was the knife-cleaner. One day, one of the knives was put on the table, not as clean as it might have been. Mr. Colburn, for this offence, tied Aaron up in the wood-house, and gave him over fifty lashes on the bare back with a cow-hide, after which, he made me wash him down with rum. This seemed to put him into more agony than the whipping. After being untied he went home to his master, and complained of the treatment which he had received. Mr. Darby would give no heed to anything he had to say, but sent him directly back. Colburn, learning that he had been to his master with complaints, tied him up again, and gave him a more severe whipping than before. The poor fellow's back was literally cut to pieces; so much so, that he was not able to work for ten or twelve days.

There was, also, among the servants, a girl whose master resided in the country. Her name was Patsey. Mr. Colburn tied her up one evening, and whipped her until several of the boarders came out and begged him to desist. The reason for whipping her was this. She was engaged to be married to a man belonging to Major William Christy, who resided four or five miles north of the city. Mr. Colburn had forbid her to see John Christy. The reason of this was said to be the regard which he himself had for Patsey. She went to meeting that evening, and John returned home with her. Mr. Colburn had intended to flog John, if he came within the inclosure; but John knew too well the temper of his rival, and kept at a safe distance:—so he took vengeance on the poor girl. If all the slave-drivers had been called together, I do not think a more cruel man than John Colburn—and he too a northern man—could have been found among them.

While living at the Missouri hotel, a circumstance occurred which caused me great unhappiness. My master sold my mother, and all her children, except myself. They were sold to different persons in the city of St. Louis.

CHAPTER III

I was soon after taken from Mr. Colburn's, and hired to Elijah P. Lovejoy,* who was at that time publisher and editor of the "St. Louis Times." My work, while with him, was mainly in the printing office, waiting on the hands, working the press, &c. Mr. Lovejoy was a very good man, and decidedly the best master that I had ever had. I am chiefly indebted to him, and to my employment in the printing office, for what little learning I obtained while in slavery.

Though slavery is thought, by some, to be mild in Missouri, when compared with the cotton, sugar and rice growing states, yet no part of our slaveholding country is more noted for the barbarity of its inhabitants than St. Louis. It was here that Col. Harney, a United States officer, whipped a slave woman to death. It was here that Francis McIntosh, a free colored man from Pittsburg, was taken from the steamboat Flora and burned at the stake. During a residence of eight years in this city, numerous cases of extreme cruelty came under my own observation; to record them all would occupy more space than could possibly be allowed in this little volume. I shall, therefore, give but a few more in addition to what I have already related.

Capt. J. B. Brant, who resided near my master, had a slave named John. He was his body servant, carriage driver, &c. On one occasion, while driving his master through the city—the streets being very muddy, and the horses going at a rapid rate—some mud spattered upon a gentleman by the name of Robert More. More was determined to be revenged. Some three or four months after this occurrence, he purchased John, for the express purpose, as he said, "to tame the d— —d nigger." After the purchase he took him to a blacksmith's shop, and had a ball and chain fastened to his leg, and then put him to driving a yoke of oxen, and kept him at hard labor, until the iron around his leg was so worn into the flesh, that it was thought mortification would ensue. In addition to this, John told me that his master whipped him regularly three times a week for the first

---

*In the memoir of Brown's life which was included with his novel *Clotel* he identified Lovejoy as the abolitionist editor who was murdered in Alton, Illinois in 1837 while defending his press against a mob. William Wells Brown, *Clotel, or the President's Daughter, a Narrative of Slave Life in the United States* (London, 1853), 4.

two months:—and all this to *"tame him."* A more noble looking man than he was not to be found in all St. Louis, before he fell into the hands of More; and a more degraded and spirit-crushed looking being was never seen on a southern plantation, after he had been subjected to this *"taming"* process for three months. The last time that I saw him, he had nearly lost the entire use of his limbs.

While living with Mr. Lovejoy, I was often sent on errands to the office of the "Missouri Republican, " published by Mr. Edward Charles. Once, while returning to the office with type, I was attacked by several large boys, sons of slave-holders, who pelted me with snow-balls. Having the heavy form of type in my hands, I could not make my escape by running; so I laid down the type and gave them battle. They gathered around me, pelting me with stones and sticks, until they overpowered me, and would have captured me, if I had not resorted to my heels. Upon my retreat they took possession of the type; and what to do to regain it I could not devise. Knowing Mr. Lovejoy to be a very humane man, I went to the office and laid the case before him. He told me to remain in the office. He took one of the apprentices with him and went after the type, and soon returned with it; but on his return informed me that Samuel McKinney had told him he would whip me, because I had hurt his boy. Soon after, McKinney was seen making his way to the office by one of the printers, who informed me of the fact, and I made my escape through the back door.

McKinney not being able to find me on his arrival, left the office in a great rage, swearing that he would whip me to death. A few days after, as I was walking along Main street, he seized me by the collar, and struck me over the head five or six times with a large cane, which caused the blood to gush from my nose and ears in such a manner that my clothes were completely saturated with blood. After beating me to his satisfaction he let me go, and I returned to the office so weak from the loss of blood that Mr. Lovejoy sent me home to my master. It was five weeks before I was able to walk again. During this time it was necessary to have some one to supply my place at the office, and I lost the situation.

After my recovery, I was hired to Capt. Otis Reynolds, as a waiter on board the steamboat Enterprise, owned by Messrs. John and Edward Walsh, commission merchants at St. Louis. This boat was then running on the upper Mississippi. My employment on board was to wait on gentlemen, and the captain being a good man, the situation was a pleasant one to me;—but in passing from place to place, and seeing new faces every day, and knowing that they could go where they pleased, I soon became unhappy, and several times thought of leaving the boat at some landing-place, and trying to make my escape to Canada, which I had heard much about as a place where the slave might live, be free, and be protected.

But whenever such thoughts would come into my mind, my resolution would soon be shaken by the remembrance that my dear mother was a slave in St. Louis, and I could not bear the idea of leaving her in that condition. She had often taken me upon her knee, and told me how she had carried me upon her back to the field when I was an infant—how often she had been whipped for leaving her work to nurse me—and how happy I would appear when she would take me into her arms. When these thoughts came over me, I would resolve never to leave the land of slavery without my mother. I thought that to leave her in slavery, after she had undergone and suffered so much for me, would be proving recreant to the duty which I owed to her. Besides this, I had three brothers and a sister there—two of my brothers having died.

My mother, my brothers Joseph and Millford, and my sister Elizabeth, belonged to Mr. Isaac Mansfield, formerly from one of the free states, (Massachusetts, I believe.) He was a tinner by trade, and carried on a large manufacturing establishment. Of all my relatives, mother was first, and sister next. One evening, while visiting them, I made some allusion to a proposed journey to Canada, and sister took her seat by my side, and taking my hand in hers, said, with tears in her eyes—

"Brother, you are not going to leave mother and your dear sister here without a friend, are you?"

I looked into her face, as the tears coursed swiftly down her cheeks, and bursting into tears myself, said—

"No, I will never desert you and mother!"

She clasped my hand in hers, and said—

"Brother, you have often declared that you would not end your days in slavery. I see no possible way in which you can escape with us; and now, brother, you are on a steamboat where there is some chance for you to escape to a land of liberty. I beseech you not to let us hinder you. If we cannot get our liberty, we do not wish to be the means of keeping you from a land of freedom."

I could restrain my feelings no longer, and an outburst of my own feelings caused her to cease speaking upon that subject. In opposition to their wishes, I pledged myself not to leave them in the hand of the oppressor. I took leave of them, and returned to the boat, and laid down in my bunk; but "sleep departed from mine eyes, and slumber from mine eyelids."

A few weeks after, on our downward passage, the boat took on board, at Hannibal, a drove of slaves, bound for the New Orleans market. They numbered from fifty to sixty, consisting of men and women from eighteen to forty years of age. A drove of slaves on a southern steamboat, bound for the cotton or sugar regions, is an occurrence so common, that no one, not even the passengers, appear to notice it, though they clank their chains at every step. There was, however, one in this gang that attracted the attention of the passengers and crew. It was a beautiful girl, apparently about twenty years of age, perfectly white, with straight light hair and blue eyes. But it was not the whiteness of her skin that created such sensation among those who gazed upon her—it was her almost unparalleled beauty. She had been on the boat but a short time, before the attention of all the passengers, including the ladies, had been called to her, and the common topic of conversation was about the beautiful slave-girl. She was not in chains. The man who claimed this article of human merchandise was a Mr. Walker—a well known slave-trader, residing in St. Louis. There was a general anxiety among the passengers and crew to learn the history of the girl. Her master kept close by her side, and it would have been considered impudent for any of the passengers to have spoken to her, and the crew were not allowed to have any conversation with them. When we reached St. Louis, the slaves were removed to a boat bound for New Orleans, and the history of the beautiful slave-girl remained a mystery.

I remained on the boat during the season, and it was not an unfrequent occurrence to have on board gangs of slaves on their way to the cotton, sugar and rice plantations of the south.

Toward the latter part of the summer Captain Reynolds left the boat, and I was sent home. I was then placed on the farm, under Mr.

Haskell, the overseer. As I had been some time out of the field, and not accustomed to work in the burning sun, it was very hard; but I was compelled to keep up with the best of the hands.

I found a great difference between the work in the steamboat cabin and that in a corn-field.

My master, who was then living in the city, soon after removed to the farm, when I was taken out of the field to work in the house as a waiter. Though his wife was very peevish, and hard to please, I much preferred to be under her control than the overseer's. They brought with them Mr. Sloane, a Presbyterian minister; Miss Martha Tulley, a niece of theirs from Kentucky; and their nephew William. The latter had been in the family a number of years, but the others were all newcomers.

Mr. Sloane was a young minister, who had been at the south but a short time, and it seemed as if his whole aim was to please the slaveholders, especially my master and mistress. He was intending to make a visit during the winter, and he not only tried to please them, but I think he succeeded admirably. When they wanted singing, he sung; when they wanted praying, he prayed; when they wanted a story told, he told a story. Instead of his teaching my master theology, my master taught theology to him. While I was with Captain Reynolds my master "got religion," and new laws were made on the plantation. Formerly we had the privilege of hunting, fishing, making splint brooms, baskets, &c., on Sunday; but this was all stopped. Every Sunday we were all compelled to attend meeting. Master was so religious that he induced some others to join him in hiring a preacher to preach to the slaves.

CHAPTER IV

My master had family worship, night and morning. At night the slaves were called in to attend; but in the mornings they had to be at their work, and master did all the praying. My master and mistress were great lovers of mint julep, and every morning, a pitcher-full was made, of which they all partook freely, not excepting little master William. After drinking freely all round, they would have family worship, and then breakfast. I cannot say but I loved the julep as well as any of them, and during prayer was always careful to seat myself close to the table where it stood, so as to help myself when they were all busily engaged in their devotions. By the time prayer was over, I was about as happy as any of them. A sad accident happened one morning. In helping myself, and at the same time keeping an eye on my old mistress, I accidentally let the pitcher fall upon the floor, breaking it in pieces, and spilling the contents. This was a bad affair for me; for as soon as prayer was over, I was taken and severely chastised.

My master's family consisted of himself, his wife, and their nephew, William Moore. He was taken into the family when only a few weeks of age. His name being that of my own, mine was changed for the purpose of giving precedence to his, though I was his senior by ten or twelve years. The plantation being four miles from the city, I had to drive the family to church. I always dreaded the approach of the Sabbath; for, during service, I was obliged to stand by the horses in the hot, broiling sun, or in the rain, just as it happened.

One Sabbath, as we were driving past the house of D. D. Page, a gentleman who owned a large baking establishment, as I was sitting upon the box of the carriage, which was very much elevated, I saw Mr. Page pursuing a slave around the yard with a long whip, cutting him at every jump. The man soon escaped from the yard, and was followed by Mr. Page. They came running past us, and the slave, perceiving that he would be overtaken, stopped suddenly, and Page stumbled over him, and falling on the stone pavement, fractured one of his legs, which crippled him for life. The same gentleman, but a short time previous, tied up a woman of his, by the name of Delphia, and whipped her nearly to death; yet he was a deacon in the Baptist church, in good and regular standing. Poor Delphia! I was well acquainted with her, and called to see her while upon her sick bed; and I shall never forget her appearance. She was a member of the same church with her master.

Soon after this, I was hired out to Mr. Walker, the same man whom I have mentioned as having carried a gang of slaves down the river on the steamboat Enterprise. Seeing me in the capacity of a steward on the boat, and thinking that I would make a good hand to take care of slaves, he determined to have me for that purpose; and finding that my master would not sell me, he hired me for the term of one year.

When I learned the fact of my having been hired to a negro speculator, or a "soul driver," as they are generally called among slaves, no one can tell my emotions. Mr. Walker had offered a high price for me, as I afterwards learned, but I suppose my master was restrained from selling me by the fact that I was a near relative of his. On entering the service of Mr. Walker, I found that my opportunity of getting to a land of liberty was gone, at least for the time being. He had a gang of slaves in readiness to start for New Orleans, and in a few days we were on our journey. I am at a loss for language to express my feelings on that occasion. Although my master had told me that he had not sold me, and Mr. Walker had told me that he had not purchased me, I did not believe them; and not until I had been to New Orleans, and was on my return, did I believe that I was not sold.

There was on the boat a large room on the lower deck, in which the slaves were kept, men and women, promiscuously—all chained two and two, and a strict watch kept that they did not get loose; for cases have occurred in which slaves have got off their chains, and made their escape at landing-places, while the boats were taking in wood;—and with all our care, we lost one woman who had been taken from her husband and children, and having no desire to live without them, in the agony of her soul jumped overboard, and drowned herself. She was not chained.

It was almost impossible to keep that part of the boat clean.

On landing at Natchez, the slaves were all carried to the slave-pen, and there kept one week, during which time several of them were sold. Mr. Walker fed his slaves well. We took on board at St. Louis several hundred pounds of bacon (smoked meat) and corn-meal, and his slaves were better fed than slaves generally were in Natchez, so far as my observation extended.

At the end of a week, we left for New Orleans, the place of our final destination, which we reached in two days. Here the slaves were placed in a negro-pen, where those who wished to purchase could call and examine them. The negro-pen is a small yard, surrounded by buildings, from fifteen to twenty feet wide, with the exception of a large gate with iron bars. The slaves are kept in the building during the night, and turned out into the yard during the day. After the best of the stock was sold at private sale at the pen, the balance were taken to the Exchange Coffee-House Auction Rooms, kept by Isaac L. McCoy, and sold at public auction. After the sale of this lot of slaves, we left New Orleans for St. Louis.

CHAPTER V

On our arrival at St. Louis I went to Dr. Young, and told him that I did not wish to live with Mr. Walker any longer. I was heart-sick at seeing my fellow-creatures bought and sold. But the Dr. had hired me for the year, and stay I must. Mr. Walker again commenced purchasing another gang of slaves. He bought a man of Colonel John O'Fallon, who resided in the suburbs of the city. This man had a wife and three children. As soon as the purchase was made, he was put in jail for safe keeping, until we should be ready to start for New Orleans. His wife visited him while there, several times, and several times when she went for that purpose was refused admittance.

In the course of eight or nine weeks Mr. Walker had his cargo of human flesh made up. There was in this lot a number of old men and women, some of them with gray locks. We left St. Louis in the steamboat Carlton, Captain Swan, bound for New Orleans. On our way down, and before we reached Rodney, the place where we made our first stop, I had to prepare the old slaves for market. I was ordered to have the old men's whiskers shaved off, and the grey hairs plucked out where they were not too numerous, in which case he had a preparation of blacking to color it, and with a blacking brush we would put it on. This was new business to me, and was performed in a room where the passengers could not see us. These slaves were also taught how old they were by Mr. Walker, and after going through the blacking process they looked ten or fifteen years younger; and I am sure that some of those who purchased slaves of Mr. Walker were dreadfully cheated, especially in the ages of the slaves which they bought.

We landed at Rodney, and the slaves were driven to the pen in the back part of the village. Several were sold at this place, during our stay of four or five days, when we proceeded to Natchez. There we landed at night, and the gang were put in the warehouse until morning, when they were driven to the pen. As soon as the slaves are put in these pens, swarms of planters may be seen in and about them. They knew when Walker was expected, as he always had the time advertised beforehand when he would be in Rodney, Natchez, and New Orleans. These were the principal places where he offered his slaves for sale.

When at Natchez the second time, I saw a slave very cruelly whipped. He belonged to a Mr. Broadwell, a merchant who kept a store on the wharf. The slave's name was Lewis. I had known him several years, as he was formerly from St. Louis. We were expecting a steamboat down the river, in which we were to take passage for New Orleans. Mr. Walker sent me to the landing to watch for the boat, ordering me to inform him on its arrival. While there I went into the store to see Lewis. I saw a slave in the store, and asked him where Lewis was. Said he, "They have got Lewis hanging between the heavens and the earth." I asked him what he meant by that. He told me to go into the warehouse and see. I went in, and found Lewis there. He was tied up to a beam, with his toes just touching the floor. As there was no one in the warehouse but himself, I inquired the reason of his being in that situation. He said Mr. Broadwell had sold his wife to a planter six miles from the city, and that he had been to visit her—that he went in the night, expecting to return before daylight, and went without his master's permission. The patrol had taken him up before he reached his wife. He was put in jail, and his master had to pay for his catching and keeping, and that was what he was tied up for.

Just as he finished his story, Mr. Broadwell came in, and inquired what I was doing there. I knew not what to say, and while I was thinking what reply to make he struck me over the head with the cowhide, the end of which struck me over my right eye, sinking deep into the flesh, leaving a scar which I carry to this day. Before I visited Lewis he had received fifty lashes. Mr. Broadwell gave him fifty lashes more after I came out, as I was afterwards informed by Lewis himself.

The next day we proceeded to New Orleans, and put the gang in the same negro-pen which we occupied before. In a short time the planters came flocking to the pen to purchase slaves. Before the slaves were exhibited for sale, they were dressed and driven out into the yard. Some were set to dancing, some to jumping, some to singing, and some to playing cards. This was done to make them appear cheerful and happy. My business was to see that they were placed in those situations before the arrival of the purchasers, and I have often set them to dancing when their cheeks were wet with tears. As slaves were in good demand at that time, they were all soon disposed of, and we again set out for St. Louis.

On our arrival, Mr. Walker purchased a farm five or six miles from the city. He had no family, but made a housekeeper of one of his female slaves. Poor Cynthia! I knew her well. She was a quadroon, and one of the most beautiful women I ever saw. She was a native of St. Louis, and bore an irreproachable character for virtue and propriety of conduct. Mr. Walker bought her for the New Orleans market, and took her down with him on one of the trips that I made with him. Never shall I forget the circumstances of that voyage! On the first night that we were on board the steamboat, he directed me to put her into a state-room he had provided for her, apart from the other slaves. I had seen too much of the workings of slavery not to know what this meant. I accordingly watched him into the state-room, and listened to hear what passed between them. I heard him make his base offers, and her reject them. He told her that if she would accept his vile proposals, he would take her back with him to St. Louis, and establish her as his housekeeper on his farm. But if she persisted in rejecting them, he would sell her as a field hand on the worst plantation on the river. Neither threats nor bribes prevailed, however, and he retired, disappointed of his prey.

The next morning poor Cynthia told me what had passed, and bewailed her sad fate with floods of tears. I comforted and encouraged her all I could; but I foresaw but too well what the result must be. Without entering into any further particulars, suffice it to say that Walker performed his part of the contract at that time. He took her back to St. Louis, established her as his mistress and housekeeper at his farm, and before I left, he had two children by her. But, mark the end! Since I have been at the North, I have been credibly informed that Walker has been married, and, as a previous measure, sold poor Cynthia and her four children (she having had two more since I came away) into hopeless bondage!

He soon commenced purchasing to make up the third gang. We took steamboat, and went to Jefferson City, a town on the Missouri river. Here we landed, and took stage for the interior of the state. He bought a number of slaves as he passed the different farms and villages. After getting twenty-two or twenty-three men and women, we arrived at St. Charles, a village on the banks of the Missouri. Here he purchased a woman who had a child in her arms, appearing to be four or five weeks old.

We had been travelling by land for some days, and were in hopes to have found a boat at this place for St. Louis, but were disappointed. As no boat was expected for some days, we started for St. Louis by land. Mr. Walker had purchased two horses. He rode one, and I the other. The slaves were chained together, and we took up our line of march, Mr. Walker taking the lead, and I bringing up the rear. Though the distance was not more than twenty miles, we did not reach it the first day. The road was worse than any that I have ever travelled.

Soon after we left St. Charles the young child grew very cross, and kept up a noise during the greater part of the day. Mr. Walker complained of its crying several times, and told the mother to stop the child's d— —d noise, or he would. The woman tried to keep the child from crying, but could not. We put up at night with an acquaintance of Mr. Walker, and in the morning, just as we were about to start, the child again commenced crying. Walker stepped up to her, and told her to give the child to him. The mother tremblingly obeyed. He took the child by one arm, as you would a cat by the leg, walked into the house, and said to the lady,

"Madam, I will make you a present of this little nigger; it keeps such a noise that I can't bear it."

"Thank you, sir," said the lady.

The mother, as soon as she saw that her child was to be left, ran up to Mr. Walker, and falling upon her knees, begged him to let her have her child; she clung around his legs, and cried, "Oh, my child! my child! master, do let me have my child! oh, do, do, do! I will stop its crying if you will only let me have it again." When I saw this woman crying for her child so piteously, a shudder—a feeling akin to horror—shot through my frame. I have often since in imagination heard her crying for her child:—

> "O, master, let me stay to catch
>   My baby's sobbing breath,
> His little glassy eye to watch,
>   And smooth his limbs in death,
>
> And cover him with grass and leaf,
>   Beneath the large oak tree:

It is not sullenness, but grief—
    O, master, pity me!

The morn was chill—I spoke no word,
    But feared my babe might die,
And heard all day, or thought I heard,
    My little baby cry.

At noon, oh, how I ran and took
    My baby to my breast!
I lingered—and the long lash broke
    My sleeping infant's rest.

I worked till night—till darkest night,
    In torture and disgrace;
Went home and watched till morning light,
    To see my baby's face.

Then give me but one little hour—
    O! do not lash me so!
One little hour—one little hour—
    And gratefully I'll go."

Mr. Walker commanded her to return into the ranks with the other slaves. Women who had children were not chained, but those that had none were. As soon as her child was disposed of she was chained in the gang.

The following song I have often heard the slaves sing, when about to be carried to the far south. It is said to have been composed by a slave.

"See these poor souls from Africa
Transported to America;
We are stolen, and sold to Georgia—
Will you go along with me?
We are stolen, and sold to Georgia—
Come sound the jubilee!

See wives and husbands sold apart,
Their children's screams will break my heart;—
There's a better day a coming—
Will you go along with me?
There's a better day a coming,
Go sound the jubilee!

O, gracious Lord! when shall it be,
That we poor souls shall all be free?
Lord, break them slavery powers—
Will you go along with me?
Lord, break them slavery powers,
Go sound the jubilee!

Dear Lord, dear Lord, when slavery 'll cease,
Then we poor souls will have our peace;—
There's a better day a coming—
Will you go along with me?
There's a better day a coming,
Go sound the jubilee!"

We finally arrived at Mr. Walker's farm. He had a house built during our absence to put slaves in. It was a kind of domestic jail. The slaves were put in the jail at night, and worked on the farm during the day. They were kept here until the gang was completed, when we again started for New Orleans, on board the steamboat North America, Capt. Alexander Scott. We had a large number of slaves in this gang. One, by the name of Joe, Mr. Walker was training up to take my place, as my time was nearly out, and glad was I. We made our first stop at Vicksburg, where we remained one week and sold several slaves.

Mr. Walker, though not a good master, had not flogged a slave since I had been with him, though he had threatened me. The slaves were kept in the pen, and he always put up at the best hotel, and kept his wines in his room, for the accommodation of those who called to negotiate with him for the purchase of slaves. One day, while we were at Vicksburg, several gentlemen came to see him for that purpose, and as usual the wine was called for. I took the tray and started around with it, and having accidentally filled some of the glasses too full, the gentlemen spilled the wine on their clothes as they went to drink. Mr. Walker apologized to them for my carelessness, but looked at me as though he would see me again on this subject.

After the gentlemen had left the room, he asked me what I meant by my carelessness, and said that he would attend to me. The next morning he gave me a note to carry to the jailer, and a dollar in money to give to him. I suspected that all was not right, so I went down near the landing, where I met with a sailor, and, walking up to him, asked him if he would be so kind as to read the note for me. He read it over, and then looked at me. I asked him to tell me what was in it. Said he,

"They are going to give you hell."

"Why?" said I.

He said, "This is a note to have you whipped, and says that you have a dollar to pay for it."

He handed me back the note, and off I started. I knew not what to do, but was determined not to be whipped. I went up to the jail—took a look at it, and walked off again. As Mr. Walker was acquainted with the jailer, I feared that I should be found out if I did not go, and be treated in consequence of it still worse.

While I was meditating on the subject, I saw a colored man about my size walk up, and the thought struck me in a moment to send him with my note. I walked up to him, and asked him who he belonged to. He said he was a free man, and had been in the city but a short time. I told him I had a note to go into the jail, and get a trunk to carry to one of the steamboats; but was so busily engaged that I could not do it, although I had a dollar to pay for it. He asked me if I would not give him the job. I handed him the note and the dollar, and off he started for the jail.

I watched to see that he went in, and as soon as I saw the door close behind him, I walked around the corner, and took my station, intending to see how my friend looked when he came out. I had been there but a short time, when a colored man came around the corner, and said to another colored man with whom he was acquainted—

"They are giving a nigger scissors in the jail."

"What for?" said the other. The man continued,

"A nigger came into the jail, and asked for the jailer. The jailer came out, and he handed him a note, and said he wanted to get a trunk. The jailer told him to go with him, and he would give him the trunk. So he took him into the room, and told the nigger to give up the dollar. He said a man had given him the dollar to pay for getting the trunk. But that lie would not answer. So they made him strip himself, and then they tied him down, and are now whipping him."

I stood by all the while listening to their talk, and soon found out that the person alluded to was my customer. I went into the street opposite the jail, and concealed myself in such a manner that I could not be seen by any one coming out. I had been there but a short time, when the young man made his appearance, and looked around for me. I, unobserved, came forth from my hiding place, behind a pile of brick, and he pretty soon saw me, and came up to me complaining bitterly, saying that I had played a trick upon him. I denied any knowledge of what the note contained, and asked him what they had done to him. He told me in substance what I heard the man tell who had come out of the jail.

"Yes," said he, "they whipped me and took my dollar, and gave me this note."

He showed me the note which the jailer had given him, telling him to give it to his master. I told him I would give him fifty cents for it—that being all the money I had. He gave it to me and took his money. He had received twenty lashes on his bare back, with the negro-whip.

I took the note and started for the hotel where I had left Mr. Walker. Upon reaching the hotel, I handed it to a stranger whom I had not seen before, and requested him to read it to me. As near as I can recollect, it was as follows:—

"Dear Sir:—By your direction, I have given your boy twenty lashes. He is a very saucy boy, and tried to make me believe that he did not belong to you, and I put it on to him well for lying to me.

"I remain

"Your obedient servant."

It is true that in most of the slave-holding cities, when a gentleman wishes his servants whipped, he can send him to the jail and have it done. Before I went in where Mr. Walker was, I wet my cheeks a little, as though I had been crying. He looked at me, and inquired what was the matter. I told him that I had never had such a whipping in my life, and handed him the note. He looked at it and laughed;—"And so you told him that you did not belong to me?" "Yes, sir," said I. "I did not know that there was any harm in that." He told me I must behave myself, if I did not want to be whipped again.

This incident shows how it is that slavery makes its victims lying and mean; for which vices it afterwards reproaches them, and uses them as arguments to prove that they deserve no better fate. Had I entertained the same views of right and wrong which I now do, I am sure I should never have practised the deception upon that poor fellow which I did. I know of no act committed by me while in slavery which I have regretted more than that; and I heartily desire that it may be at some time or other in my power to make him amends for his vicarious sufferings in my behalf.

CHAPTER VI

In a few days we reached New Orleans, and arriving there in the night, remained on board until morning. While at New Orleans this time, I saw a slave killed; an account of which has been published by Theodore D. Weld, in his book entitled "Slavery as it is."* The circumstances were as follows. In the evening, between seven and eight o'clock, a slave came running down the levee, followed by several men and boys. The whites were crying out, "Stop that nigger! stop that nigger!" while the poor panting slave, in almost breathless accents, was repeating, "I did not steal the meat—I did not steal the meat." The poor man at last took refuge in the river. The whites who were in pursuit of him, run on board of one of the boats to see if they could discover him. They finally espied him under the bow of the steamboat Trenton. They got a pike-pole, and tried to drive him from his hiding place. When they would strike at him he would dive under the water. The water was so cold, that it soon became evident that he must come out or be drowned.

While they were trying to drive him from under the bow of the boat or drown him, he would in broken and imploring accents say, "I did not steal the meat; I did not steal the meat. My master lives up the river. I want to see my master. I did not steal the meat. Do let me go home to master." After punching him, and striking him over the head for some time, he at last sunk in the water, to rise no more alive.

On the end of the pike-pole with which they were striking him was a hook, which caught in his clothing, and they hauled him up on the bow of the boat. Some said he was dead; others said he was *"playing possum;"* while others kicked him to make him get up; but it was of no use—he was dead.

As soon as they became satisfied of this, they commenced leaving, one after another. One of the hands on the boat informed the captain that they had killed the man, and that the dead body was lying on the deck. The captain came on deck, and said to those who

---

*Theodore D. Weld, *Slavery As It Is: Testimony of a Thousand Witnesses* (New York, 1839) included numerous clippings of incidents involving slaves from various southern newspapers.

were remaining, "You have killed this nigger; now take him off of my boat." The captain's name was Hart. The dead body was dragged on shore and left there. I went on board of the boat where our gang of slaves were, and during the whole night my mind was occupied with what I had seen. Early in the morning I went on shore to see if the dead body remained there. I found it in the same position that it was left the night before. I watched to see what they would do with it. It was left there until between eight and nine o'clock, when a cart, which takes up the trash out of the streets, came along, and the body was thrown in, and in a few minutes more was covered over with dirt which they were removing from the streets. During the whole time, I did not see more than six or seven persons around it, who, from their manner, evidently regarded it as no uncommon occurrence.

During our stay in the city I met with a young white man with whom I was well acquainted in St. Louis. He had been sold into slavery, under the following circumstances. His father was a drunkard, and very poor, with a family of five or six children. The father died, and left the mother to take care of and provide for the children as best she might. The eldest was a boy, named Burrill, about thirteen years of age, who did chores in a store kept by Mr. Riley, to assist his mother in procuring a living for the family. After working with him two years, Mr. Riley took him to New Orleans to wait on him while in that city on a visit, and when he returned to St. Louis, he told the mother of the boy that he had died with the yellow fever. Nothing more was heard from him, no one supposing him to be alive. I was much astonished when Burrill told me his story. Though I sympathized with him I could not assist him. We were both slaves. He was poor, uneducated, and without friends; and, if living, is, I presume, still held as a slave.

After selling out his cargo of human flesh, we returned to St. Louis, and my time was up with Mr. Walker. I had served him one year, and it was the longest year I ever lived.

CHAPTER VII

I was sent home, and was glad enough to leave the service of one who was tearing the husband from the wife, the child from the mother, and the sister from the brother—but a trial more severe and heart-rending than any which I had yet met with awaited me. My dear sister had been sold to a man who was going to Natchez, and was lying in jail awaiting the hour of his departure. She had expressed her determination to die, rather than go to the far south, and she was put in jail for safekeeping. I went to the jail the same day that I arrived, but as the jailer was not in I could not see her.

I went home to my master, in the country, and the first day after my return he came where I was at work, and spoke to me very politely. I knew from his appearance that something was the matter. After talking to me about my several journeys to New Orleans with Mr. Walker, he told me that he was hard pressed for money, and as he had sold my mother and all her children except me, he thought it would be better to sell me than any other one, and that as I had been used to living in the city, he thought it probable that I would prefer it to country life. I raised up my head, and looked him full in the face. When my eyes caught his he immediately looked to the ground. After a short pause, I said,

"Master, mother has often told me that you are a near relative of mine, and I have often heard you admit the fact; and after you have hired me out, and received, as I once heard you say, nine hundred dollars for my services—after receiving this large sum, will you sell me to be carried to New Orleans or some other place?"

"No," said he, "I do not intend to sell you to a negro trader. If I had wished to have done that, I might have sold you to Mr. Walker for a large sum, but I would not sell you to a negro trader. You may go to the city, and find you a good master."

"But," said I, "I cannot find a good master in the whole city of St. Louis."

"Why?" said he.

"Because there are no good masters in the state."

"Do you not call me a good master?"

"If you were you would not sell me."

"Now I will give you one week to find a master in, and surely you can do it in that time."

The price set by my evangelical master upon my soul and body was the trifling sum of five hundred dollars. I tried to enter into some arrangement by which I might purchase my freedom; but he would enter into no such arrangement.

I set out for the city with the understanding that I was to return in a week with some one to become my new master. Soon after reaching the city, I went to the jail, to learn if I could once more see my sister; but could not gain admission. I then went to mother, and learned from her that the owner of my sister intended to start for Natchez in a few days.

I went to the jail again the next day, and Mr. Simonds, the keeper, allowed me to see my sister for the last time. I cannot give a just description of the scene at that parting interview. Never, never can be erased from my heart the occurrences of that day! When I entered the room where she was, she was seated in one corner, alone. There were four other women in the same room, belonging to the same man. He had purchased them, he said, for his own use. She was seated with her face towards the door where I entered, yet she did not look up until I walked up to her. As soon as she observed me she sprung up, threw her arms around my neck, leaned her head upon my breast, and, without uttering a word, burst into tears. As soon as she recovered herself sufficiently to speak, she advised me to take mother, and try to get out of slavery. She said there was no hope for herself—that she must live and die a slave. After giving her some advice, and taking from my finger a ring and placing it upon hers, I bade her farewell forever, and returned to my mother, and then and there made up my mind to leave for Canada as soon as possible.

I had been in the city nearly two days, and as I was to be absent only a week, I thought best to get on my journey as soon as possible. In conversing with mother, I found her unwilling to make the attempt to reach a land of liberty, but she counselled me to get my liberty if I could. She said, as all her children were in slavery, she did not wish to leave them. I could not bear the idea of leaving her among those pirates, when there was a prospect of being able to get away from them. After much persuasion I succeeded in inducing her to make the attempt to get away.

The time fixed for our departure was the next night. I had with me a little money that I had received, from time to time, from gentlemen for whom I had done errands. I took my scanty means and purchased some dried beef, crackers and cheese, which I carried to mother, who had provided herself with a bag to carry it in. I occasionally thought of my old master, and of my mission to the city to find a new one. I waited with the most intense anxiety for the appointed time to leave the land of slavery, in search of a land of liberty.

The time at length arrived, and we left the city just as the clock struck nine. We proceeded to the upper part of the city, where I had been two or three times during the day, and selected a skiff to carry us across the river. The boat was not mine, nor did I know to whom it did belong; neither did I care. The boat was fastened with a small pole, which, with the aid of a rail, I soon loosened from its moorings. After hunting round and finding a board to use as an oar, I turned to the city, and bidding it a long farewell, pushed off my boat. The current running very swift, we had not reached the middle of the stream before we were directly opposite the city.

We were soon upon the Illinois shore, and, leaping from the boat, turned it adrift, and the last I saw of it it was going down the river at good speed. We took the main road to Alton, and passed through just at daylight, when we made for the woods, where we remained during the day. Our reason for going into the woods was, that we expected that Mr. Mansfield (the man who owned my mother) would start in pursuit of her as soon as he discovered that she was missing. He also knew that I had been in the city looking for a new master, and we thought probably he would go out to my master's to see if he could find my mother, and in so doing, Dr. Young might be led to suspect that I had gone to Canada to find a purchaser.

We remained in the woods during the day, and as soon as darkness overshadowed the earth, we started again on our gloomy way, having no guide but the NORTH STAR. We continued to travel by night, and secrete ourselves in the woods by day; and every night, before emerging from our hidingplace, we would anxiously look for our friend and leader—the NORTH STAR. And in the language of Pierpont* we might have exclaimed,

---

*John Pierpont (1785—1866) was a clergyman, reformer and abolitionist poet.

"Star of the North! while blazing day
Pours round me its full tide of light,
And hides thy pale but faithful ray,
I, too, lie hid, and long for night.
For night;—I dare not walk at noon,
Nor dare I trust the faithless moon,
Nor faithless man, whose burning lust
For gold hath riveted my chain;
No other leader can I trust
But thee, of even the starry train;
For, all the host around thee burning,
Like faithless man, keep turning, turning.

In the dark top of southern pines
I nestled, when the driver's horn
Called to the field, in lengthening lines,
My fellows, at the break of morn.
And there I lay, till thy sweet face
Looked in upon my 'hiding place,'
Star of the North!
Thy light, that no poor slave deceiveth,
Shall set me free."

CHAPTER VIII

As we travelled towards a land of liberty, my heart would at times leap for joy. At other times, being, as I was, almost constantly on my feet, I felt as though I could travel no further. But when I thought of slavery, with its democratic whips—its republican chains—its evangelical blood-hounds, and its religious slave-holders—when I thought of all this paraphernalia of American democracy and religion behind me, and the prospect of liberty before me, I was encouraged to press forward, my heart was strengthened, and I forgot that I was tired or hungry.

On the eighth day of our journey, we had a very heavy rain, and in a few hours after it commenced we had not a dry thread upon our bodies. This made our journey still more unpleasant. On the tenth day, we found ourselves entirely destitute of provisions, and how to obtain any we could not tell. We finally resolved to stop at some farmhouse, and try to get something to eat. We had no sooner determined to do this, than we went to a house, and asked them for some food. We were treated with great kindness, and they not only gave us something to eat, but gave us provisions to carry with us. They advised us to travel by day and lie by at night. Finding ourselves about one hundred and fifty miles from St. Louis, we concluded that it would be safe to travel by daylight, and did not leave the house until the next morning. We travelled on that day through a thickly settled country, and through one small village. Though we were fleeing from a land of oppression, our hearts were still there. My dear sister and two beloved brothers were behind us, and the idea of giving them up, and leaving them forever, made us feel sad. But with all this depression of heart, the thought that I should one day be free, and call my body my own, buoyed me up, and made my heart leap for joy. I had just been telling my mother how I should try to get employment as soon as we reached Canada, and how I intended to purchase us a little farm, and how I would earn money enough to buy sister and brothers, and how happy we would be in our own FREE HOME—when three men came up on horseback, and ordered us to stop.

I turned to the one who appeared to be the principal man, and asked him what he wanted. He said he had a warrant to take us up.

The three immediately dismounted, and one took from his pocket a handbill, advertising us as runaways, and offering a reward of two hundred dollars for our apprehension and delivery in the city of St. Louis. The advertisement had been put out by Isaac Mansfield and John Young.

While they were reading the advertisement, mother looked me in the face, and burst into tears. A cold chill ran over me, and such a sensation I never experienced before, and I hope never to again. They took out a rope and tied me, and we were taken back about six miles, to the house of the individual who appeared to be the leader. We reached there about seven o'clock in the evening, had supper, and were separated for the night. Two men remained in the room during the night. Before the family retired to rest, they were all called together to attend prayers. The man who but a few hours before had bound my hands together with a strong cord, read a chapter from the Bible, and then offered up prayer, just as though God had sanctioned the act he had just committed upon a poor, panting, fugitive slave.

The next morning a blacksmith came in, and put a pair of handcuffs on me, and we started on our journey back to the land of whips, chains and Bibles. Mother was not tied, but was closely watched at night. We were carried back in a wagon, and after four days' travel, we came in sight of St. Louis. I cannot describe my feelings upon approaching the city.

As we were crossing the ferry, Mr. Wiggins, the owner of the ferry, came up to me, and inquired what I had been doing that I was in chains. He had not heard that I had run away. In a few minutes we were on the Missouri side, and were taken directly to the jail. On the way thither, I saw several of my friends, who gave me a nod of recognition as I passed them. After reaching the jail, we were locked up in different apartments.

CHAPTER IX

I had been in jail but a short time when I heard that my master was sick, and nothing brought more joy to my heart than that intelligence. I prayed fervently for him—not for his recovery, but for his death. I knew he would be exasperated at having to pay for my apprehension, and knowing his cruelty, I feared him. While in jail, I learned that my sister Elizabeth, who was in prison when we left the city, had been carried off four days before our arrival.

I had been in jail but a few hours when three negro-traders, learning that I was secured thus for running away, came to my prison-house and looked at me, expecting that I would be offered for sale. Mr. Mansfield, the man who owned mother, came into the jail as soon as Mr. Jones, the man who arrested us, informed him that he had brought her back. He told her that he would not whip her, but would sell her to a negro-trader, or take her to New Orleans himself. After being in jail about one week, master sent a man to take me out of jail, and send me home. I was taken out and carried home, and the old man was well enough to sit up. He had me brought into the room where he was, and as I entered, he asked me where I had been? I told him I had acted according to his orders. He had told me to look for a master, and I had been to look for one. He answered that he did not tell me to go to Canada to look for a master. I told him that as I had served him faithfully, and had been the means of putting a number of hundreds of dollars into his pocket, I thought I had a right to my liberty. He said he had promised my father that I should not be sold to supply the New Orleans market, or he would sell me to a negro-trader.

I was ordered to go into the field to work, and was closely watched by the overseer during the day, and locked up at night. The overseer gave me a severe whipping on the second day that I was in the field. I had been at home but a short time, when master was able to ride to the city; and on his return he informed me that he had sold me to Samuel Willi, a merchant tailor. I knew Mr. Willi. I had lived with him three or four months some years before, when he hired me of my master.

Mr. Willi was not considered by his servants as a very bad man, nor was he the best of masters. I went to my new home, and found my

33

new mistress very glad to see me. Mr. Willi owned two servants before he purchased me—Robert and Charlotte. Robert was an excellent white-washer, and hired his time from his master, paying him one dollar per day, besides taking care of himself. He was known in the city by the name of Bob Music. Charlotte was an old woman, who attended to the cooking, washing, &c. Mr. Willi was not a wealthy man, and did not feel able to keep many servants around his house; so he soon decided to hire me out, and as I had been accustomed to service in steamboats, he gave me the privilege of finding such employment.

I soon secured a situation on board the steamer Otto, Capt. J. B. Hill, which sailed from St. Louis to Independence, Missouri. My former master, Dr. Young, did not let Mr. Willi know that I had run away, or he would not have permitted me to go on board a steamboat. The boat was not quite ready to commence running, and therefore I had to remain with Mr. Willi. But during this time, I had to undergo a trial for which I was entirely unprepared. My mother, who had been in jail since her return until the present time, was now about being carried to New Orleans, to die on a cotton, sugar, or rice plantation!

I had been several times to the jail, but could obtain no interview with her. I ascertained, however, the time the boat in which she was to embark would sail, and as I had not seen mother since her being thrown into prison, I felt anxious for the hour of sailing to come. At last, the day arrived when I was to see her for the first time after our painful separation, and, for aught that I knew, for the last time in this world!

At about ten o'clock in the morning I went on board of the boat, and found her there in company with fifty or sixty other slaves. She was chained to another woman. On seeing me, she immediately dropped her head upon her heaving bosom. She moved not, neither did she weep. Her emotions were too deep for tears. I approached, threw my arms around her neck, kissed her, and fell upon my knees, begging her forgiveness, for I thought myself to blame for her sad condition; for if I had not persuaded her to accompany me, she would not then have been in chains.

She finally raised her head, looked me in the face, (and such a look none but an angel can give!) and said, *"My dear son, you are not to blame for my being here. You have done nothing more nor less than your duty. Do not, I pray you, weep for me. I cannot last long upon a cotton plantation. I feel that my heavenly Master will soon call me home, and then I shall be out of the hands of the slave-holders!"*

I could bear no more—my heart struggled to free itself from the human form. In a moment she saw Mr. Mansfield coming toward that part of the boat, and she whispered into my ear, *"My child, we must soon part to meet no more this side of the grave. You have ever said that you would not die a slave; that you would be a freeman. Now try to get your liberty! You will soon have no one to look after but yourself!"* and just as she whispered the last sentence into my ear, Mansfield came up to me, and with an oath, said, "Leave here this instant; you have been the means of my losing one hundred dollars to get this wench back"—at the same time kicking me with a heavy pair of boots. As I left her, she gave one shriek, saying, "God be with you!" It was the last time that I saw her, and the last word I heard her utter.

I walked on shore. The bell was tolling. The boat was about to start. I stood with a heavy heart, waiting to see her leave the wharf. As I thought of my mother, I could but feel that I had lost

> "— — the glory of my life,
> My blessing and my pride!
> I half forgot the name of slave,
> When she was by my side."

The love of liberty that had been burning in my bosom had well-nigh gone out. I felt as though I was ready to die. The boat moved gently from the wharf, and while she glided down the river, I realized that my mother was indeed

> "Gone—gone—sold and gone,
> To the rice swamp, dank and lone!"

After the boat was out of sight I returned home; but my thoughts were so absorbed in what I had witnessed, that I knew not what I was about half of the time. Night came, but it brought no sleep to my eyes.

In a few days, the boat upon which I was to work being ready, I went on board to commence. This employment suited me better than living in the city, and I remained until the close of navigation; though it proved anything but pleasant. The captain was a drunken, profligate, hard-hearted creature, not knowing how to treat himself, or any other person.

The boat, on its second trip, brought down Mr. Walker, the man of whom I have spoken in a previous chapter, as hiring my time. He had between one and two hundred slaves, chained and manacled. Among them was a man that formerly belonged to my old master's brother, Aaron Young. His name was Solomon. He was a preacher, and belonged to the same church with his master. I was glad to see the old man. He wept like a child when he told me how he had been sold from his wife and children.

The boat carried down, while I remained on board, four or five gangs of slaves. Missouri, though a comparatively new state, is very much engaged in raising slaves to supply the southern market. In a former chapter, I have mentioned that I was once in the employ of a slave-trader, or driver, as he is called at the south. For fear that some may think that I have misrepresented a slave-driver, I will here give an extract from a paper published in a slave-holding state, Tennessee, called the "Millennial Trumpeter."

"Droves of negroes, chained together in dozens and scores, and hand-cuffed, have been driven through our country in numbers far surpassing any previous year, and these vile slave-drivers and dealers are swarming like buzzards around a carrion. Through this county, you cannot pass a few miles in the great roads without having every feeling of humanity insulted and lacerated by this spectacle, nor can you go into any county or any neighborhood, scarely, without seeing or hearing of some of these despicable creatures, called negro-drivers.

"Who is a negro-driver? One whose eyes dwell with delight on lacerated bodies of helpless men, women and children; whose soul feels diabolical raptures at the chains, and hand-cuffs, and cart-whips, for inflicting tortures on weeping mothers torn from helpless babes, and on husbands and wives torn asunder forever!"

Dark and revolting as is the picture here drawn, it is from the pen of one living in the midst of slavery. But though these men may cant about negro-drivers, and tell what despicable creatures they are, who is it, I ask, that supplies them with the human beings that they are tearing asunder? I answer, as far as I have any knowledge of the state where I came from, that those who raise slaves for the market are to be found among all classes, from Thomas H. Benton down to the lowest political demagogue who may be able to purchase a woman for the purpose of raising stock, and from the doctor of divinity down to the most humble lay member in the church.

It was not uncommon in St. Louis to pass by an auction-stand, and behold a woman upon the auction-block, and hear the seller crying out, *"How much is offered for this woman? She is a good cook, good washer, a good obedient servant. She has got religion!"* Why should this man tell the purchasers that she has religion? I answer, because in Missouri, and as far as I have any knowledge of slavery in the other states, the religious teaching consists in teaching the slave that he must never strike a white man; that God made him for a slave; and that, when whipped, he must not find fault—for the Bible says, "He that knoweth his master's will and doeth it not, shall be beaten with many stripes!" And slaver-holders find such religion very profitable to them.

After leaving the steamer Otto, I resided at home, in Mr. Willi's family, and again began to lay my plans for making my escape from slavery. The anxiety to be a freeman would not let me rest day or night. I would think of the northern cities that I had heard so much about;—of Canada, where so many of my acquaintances had found a refuge. I would dream at night that I was in Canada, a freeman, and on waking in the morning, weep to find myself so sadly mistaken.

> "I would think of Victoria's domain,
>   And in a moment I seemed to be there!
> But the fear of being taken again,
>   Soon hurried me back to despair."

Mr. Willi treated me better than Dr. Young ever had; but instead of making me contented and happy, it only rendered me the more miserable, for it enabled me better to appreciate liberty. Mr. Willi was a man who loved money as most men do, and without looking for an opportunity to sell me, he found one in the offer of Captain Enoch Price, a steamboat owner and commission merchant, living in the city of St. Louis. Captain Price tendered seven hundred dollars, which was two hundred more than Mr. Willi had paid. He therefore thought best to accept the offer. I was wanted for a carriage driver, and Mrs. Price was very much pleased with the captain's bargain. His family consisted besides of one child. He had three servants besides myself—one man and two women.

Mrs. Price was very proud of her servants, always keeping them well dressed, and as soon as I had been purchased, she resolved to have a new carriage. And soon one was procured, and all preparations were made for a turn-out in grand style, I being the driver.

One of the female servants was a girl some eighteen or twenty years of age, named Maria. Mrs. Price was very soon determined to have us united, if she could so arrange matters. She would often urge upon me the necessity of having a wife, saying that it would be so pleasant for me to take one in the same family! But getting married, while in slavery, was the last of my thoughts; and had I been ever so inclined, I should not have married Maria, as my love had already gone in another quarter. Mrs. Price soon found out that her efforts at this match-making between Maria and myself would not prove successful. She also discovered (or thought she had) that I was rather partial to a girl named Eliza, who was owned by Dr. Mills. This induced her at once to endeavor the purchase of Eliza, so great was her desire to get me a wife!

Before making the attempt, however, she deemed it best to talk to me a little upon the subject of love, courtship, and marriage. Accordingly, one afternoon she called me into her room—telling me to take a chair and sit down. I did so, thinking it rather strange, for servants are not very often asked thus to sit down in the same room with the master or mistress. She said that she had found out that I did not care enough about Maria to marry her. I told her that was true. She then asked me if there was not a girl in the city that I loved. Well, now, this was coming into too close quarters with me! People, generally, don't like to tell their love stories to everybody that may think fit to ask about them, and it was so with me. But, after blushing a while and recovering myself, I told her that I did not want a wife. She then asked me if I did not think something of Eliza. I told her that I did. She then said that if I wished to marry Eliza, she would purchase her if she could.

I gave but little encouragement to this proposition, as I was determined to make another trial to get my liberty, and I knew that if I should have a wife, I should not be willing to leave her behind; and if I should attempt to bring her with me, the chances would be difficult for success. However, Eliza was purchased, and brought into the family.

CHAPTER X

But the more I thought of the trap laid by Mrs. Price to make me satisfied with my new home, by getting me a wife, the more I determined never to marry any woman on earth until I should get my liberty. But this secret I was compelled to keep to myself, which placed me in a very critical position. I must keep upon good terms with Mrs. Price and Eliza. I therefore promised Mrs. Price that I would marry Eliza; but said that I was not then ready. And I had to keep upon good terms with Eliza, for fear that Mrs. Price would find out that I did not intend to get married.

I have here spoken of marriage, and it is very common among slaves themselves to talk of it. And it is common for slaves to be married; or at least to have the marriage ceremony performed. But there is no such thing as slaves being lawfully married. There has never yet a case occurred where a slave has been tried for bigamy. The man may have as many women as he wishes, and the women as many men; and the law takes no cognizance of such acts among slaves. And in fact some masters, when they have sold the husband from the wife, compel her to take another.

There lived opposite Captain Price's, Doctor Farrar, well known in St. Louis. He sold a man named Ben, to one of the traders. He also owned Ben's wife, and in a few days he compelled Sally (that was her name) to marry Peter, another man belonging to him. I asked Sally "why she married Peter so soon after Ben was sold." She said, "because master made her do it."

Mr. John Calvert, who resided near our place, had a woman named Lavinia. She was quite young, and a man to whom she was about to be married was sold, and carried into the country near St. Charles, about twenty miles from St. Louis. Mr. Calvert wanted her to get a husband; but she had resolved not to marry any other man, and she refused. Mr. Calvert whipped her in such a manner that it was thought she would die. Some of the citizens had him arrested, but it was soon hushed up. And that was the last of it. The woman did not die, but it would have been the same if she had.

Captain Price purchased me in the month of October, and I remained with him until December, when the family made a voyage to New Orleans, in a boat owned by himself, and named the

"Chester." I served on board as one of the stewards. On arriving at New Orleans, about the middle of the month, the boat took in freight for Cincinnati; and it was decided that the family should go up the river in her, and what was of more interest to me, I was to accompany them.

The long looked for opportunity to make my escape from slavery was near at hand.

Captain Price had some fears as to the propriety of taking me near a free state, or a place where it was likely I could run away, with a prospect of liberty. He asked me if I had ever been in a free state. "Oh yes," said I, "I have been in Ohio; my master carried me into that state once, but I never liked a free state."

It was soon decided that it would be safe to take me with them, and what made it more safe, Eliza was on the boat with us, and Mrs. Price, to try me, asked if I thought as much as ever of Eliza. I told her that Eliza was very dear to me indeed, and that nothing but death should part us. It was the same as if we were married. This had the desired effect. The boat left New Orleans, and proceeded up the river.

I had at different times obtained little sums of money, which I had reserved for a "rainy day." I procured some cotton cloth, and made me a bag to carry provisions in. The trials of the past were all lost in hopes for the future. The love of liberty, that had been burning in my bosom for years, and had been well-nigh extinguished, was now resuscitated. At night, when all around was peaceful, I would walk the decks, meditating upon my happy prospects.

I should have stated, that, before leaving St. Louis, I went to an old man named Frank, a slave, owned by a Mr. Sarpee. This old man was very distinguished (not only among the slave population, but also the whites) as a fortune-teller. He was about seventy years of age, something over six feet high, and very slender. Indeed, he was so small around his body, that it looked as though it was not strong enough to hold up his head.

Uncle Frank was a very great favorite with the young ladies, who would go to him in great numbers to get their fortunes told. And it was generally believed that he could really penetrate into the mysteries of futurity. Whether true or not, he had the *name,* and that is about half of what one needs in this gullible age. I found Uncle

Frank seated in the chimney corner, about ten o'clock at night. As soon as I entered, the old man left his seat. I watched his movement as well as I could by the dim light of the fire. He soon lit a lamp, and coming up, looked me full in the face, saying, "Well, my son, you have come to get uncle to tell your fortune, have you?" "Yes," said I. But how the old man should know what I came for, I could not tell. However, I paid the fee of twenty-five cents, and he commenced by looking into a gourd, filled with water. Whether the old man was a prophet, or the son of a prophet, I cannot say; but there is one thing certain, many of his predictions were verified.

I am no believer in soothsaying; yet I am sometimes at a loss to know how Uncle Frank could tell so accurately what would occur in the future. Among the many things he told was one which was enough to pay me for all the trouble of hunting him up. It was that I *should be free!* He further said, that in trying to get my liberty I would meet with many severe trials. I thought to myself any fool could tell me that!

The first place in which we landed in a free state was Cairo, a small village at the mouth of the Ohio river. We remained here but a few hours, when we proceeded to Louisville. After unloading some of the cargo, the boat started on her upward trip. The next day was the first of January. I had looked forward to New Year's day as the commencement of a new era in the history of my life. I had decided upon leaving the peculiar institution that day.

During the last night that I served in slavery I did not close my eyes a single moment. When not thinking of the future, my mind dwelt on the past. The love of a dear mother, a dear sister, and three dear brothers, yet living, caused me to shed many tears. If I could only have been assured of their being dead, I should have felt satisfied; but I imagined I saw my dear mother in the cotton-field, followed by a merciless taskmaster, and no one to speak a consoling word to her! I beheld my dear sister in the hands of a slave-driver, and compelled to submit to his cruelty! None but one placed in such a situation can for a moment imagine the intense agony to which these reflections subjected me.

CHAPTER XI

At last the time for action arrived. The boat landed at a point which appeared to me the place of all others to start from. I found that it would be impossible to carry anything with me but what was upon my person. I had some provisions, and a single suit of clothes, about half worn. When the boat was discharging her cargo, and the passengers engaged carrying their baggage on and off shore, I improved the opportunity to convey myself with my little effects on land. Taking up a trunk, I went up the wharf, and was soon out of the crowd. I made directly for the woods, where I remained until night, knowing well that I could not travel, even in the state of Ohio, during the day, without danger of being arrested.

I had long since made up my mind that I would not trust myself in the hands of any man, white or colored. The slave is brought up to look upon every white man as an enemy to him and his race; and twenty-one years in slavery had taught me that there were traitors, even among colored people. After dark, I emerged from the woods into a narrow path, which led me into the main travelled road. But I knew not which way to go. I did not know north from south, east from west. I looked in vain for the North Star; a heavy cloud hid it from my view. I walked up and down the road until near midnight, when the clouds disappeared, and I welcomed the sight of my friend—truly the slave's friend—the North Star!

As soon as I saw it, I knew my course, and before daylight I travelled twenty or twenty-five miles. It being in the winter, I suffered intensely from the cold; being without an overcoat, and my other clothes rather thin for the season. I was provided with a tinder-box, so that I could make up a fire when necessary. And but for this, I should certainly have frozen to death; for I was determined not to go to any house for shelter. I knew of a man belonging to Gen. Ashly, of St. Louis, who had run away near Cincinnati, on the way to Washington, but had been caught and carried back into slavery; and I felt that a similar fate awaited me, should I be seen by any one. I travelled at night, and lay by during the day.

On the fourth day my provisions gave out, and then what to do I could not tell. Have something to eat I must; but how to get it was the question! On the first night after my food was gone, I went to a barn on the road-side and there found some ears of corn. I took ten or twelve of them, and kept on my journey. During the next day, while in the woods, I roasted my corn and feasted upon it, thanking God that I was so well provided for.

My escape to a land of freedom now appeared certain, and the prospects of the future occupied a great part of my thoughts. What should be my occupation, was a subject of much anxiety to me; and the next thing what should be my name? I have before stated that my old master, Dr. Young, had no children of his own, but had with him a nephew, the son of his brother, Benjamin Young. When this boy was brought to Dr. Young, his name being William, the same as mine, my mother was ordered to change mine to something else. This, at the time, I thought to be one of the most cruel acts that could be committed upon my rights; and I received several very severe whippings for telling people that my name was William, after orders were given to change it. Though young, I was old enough to place a high appreciation upon my name. It was decided, however, to call me "Sandford," and this name I was known by, not only upon my master's plantation, but up to the time that I made my escape. I was sold under the name of Sandford.

But as soon as the subject came to my mind, I resolved on adopting my old name of William, and let Sandford go by the board, for I always hated it. Not because there was anything peculiar in the name; but because it had been forced upon me. It is sometimes common, at the south, for slaves to take the name of their masters. Some have a legitimate right to do so. But I always detested the idea of being called by the name of either of my masters. And as for my father, I would rather have adopted the name of "Friday," and been known as the servant of some Robinson Crusoe, than to have taken his name. So I was not only hunting for my liberty, but also hunting for a name; though I regarded the latter as of little consequence, if I could but gain the former. Travelling along the road, I would sometimes speak to myself, sounding my name over, by way of getting used to it, before I should arrive among civilized human beings. On the fifth or six day, it rained very fast, and froze about as fast as it fell, so that my clothes were one glare of ice. I travelled on at night until I became so chilled and benumbed—the wind blowing into my face—that I found it impossible to go any further, and accordingly took shelter in a barn, where I was obliged to walk about to keep from freezing.

I have ever looked upon that night as the most eventful part of my escape from slavery. Nothing but the providence of God, and that old barn, saved me from freezing to death. I received a very severe cold, which settled upon my lungs, and from time to time my feet had been frostbitten, so that it was with difficulty I could walk. In this situation I travelled two days, when I found that I must seek shelter somewhere, or die.

The thought of death was nothing frightful to me, compared with that of being caught, and again carried back into slavery. Nothing but the prospect of enjoying liberty could have induced me to undergo such trials, for

> "Behind I left the whips and chains,
> Before me were sweet Freedom's plains!"

This, and this alone, cheered me onward. But I at last resolved to seek protection from the inclemency of the weather, and therefore I secured myself behind some logs and brush, intending to wait there until some one should pass by; for I thought it probable that I might see some colored person, or, if not, some one who was not a slave-holder; for I had an idea that I should know a slave-holder as far as I could see him.

The first person that passed was a man in a buggy-wagon. He looked too genteel for me to hail him. Very soon another passed by on horseback. I attempted to speak to him, but fear made my voice fail me. As he passed, I left my hidingplace and was approaching the road, when I observed an old man walking towards me, leading a white horse. He had on a broad-brimmed hat and a very long coat, and was evidently walking for exercise. As soon as I saw him, and observed his dress, I thought to myself, "You are the man that I have been looking for!" Nor was I mistaken. He was the very man!

On approaching me, he asked me, "if I was not a slave." I looked at him some time, and then asked him "if he knew of any one who would help me, as I was sick." He answered that he would; but again asked, if I was not a slave. I told him I was. He then said that I was in a very pro-slavery neighborhood, and if I would wait until he went home, he would get a covered wagon for me. I promised to remain. He mounted his horse, and was soon out of sight.

After he was gone, I meditated whether to wait or not; being apprehensive that he had gone for some one to arrest me. But I finally concluded to remain until he should return; removing some few rods to watch his movements. After a suspense of an hour and a half or more, he returned with a two-horse covered wagon, such as are usually seen under the shed of a Quaker meetinghouse on Sundays and Thursdays; for the old man proved to be a Quaker of the George Fox stamp.

He took me to his house, but it was some time before I could be induced to enter it; not until the old lady came out, did I venture into the house. I thought I saw something in the old lady's cap that told me I was not only safe, welcome, in her house. I was not, however, prepared to receive their hospitalities. The only fault I found with them was their being too kind. I had never had a white man treat me as an equal, and the idea of a white lady waiting on me at the table was still worse! Though the table was loaded with the good things of this life, I could not eat. I thought if I could only be allowed the privilege of eating in the kitchen I should be more than satisfied!

Finding that I could not eat, the old lady, who was a "Thompsonian,"* made me a cup of "composition," or "number six;" but it was so strong and hot, that I called it *"number seven!"* However, I soon found myself at home in this family. On different occasions, when telling these facts, I have been asked how I felt upon finding myself regarded as a man by a white family; especially just having run away from one. I cannot say that I have ever answered the question yet.

The fact that I was in all probability a freeman, sounded in my ears like a charm. I am satisfied that none but a slave could place such an appreciation upon liberty as I did at that time. I wanted to see mother and sister, that I might tell them "I was free!" I wanted to see my fellow-slaves in St. Louis, and let them know that the chains were no longer upon my limbs. I wanted to see Captain Price, and let him learn from my own lips that I was no more a chattel, but a man! I was anxious, too, thus to inform Mrs. Price that she must

---

*A system of medicine named for Samuel Thomson (1769–1843) who advocated the exclusive use of vegetable drugs in treating disease. See Francis R. Packard, *History of Medicine in the United States* (2 vols., New York and London, 1963), II:1233–1239.

get another coachman. And I wanted to see Eliza more than I did either Mr. or Mrs. Price!

The fact that I was a freeman—could walk, talk, eat and sleep, as a man, and no one to stand over me with the blood-clotted cow-hide—all this made me feel that I was not myself.

The kind friend that had taken me in was named Wells Brown.* He was a devoted friend of the slave; but was very old, and not in the enjoyment of good health. After being by the fire awhile, I found that my feet had been very much frozen. I was seized with a fever, which threatened to confine me to my bed. But my Thompsonian friends soon raised me, treating me as kindly as if I had been one of their own children. I remained with them twelve or fifteen days, during which time they made me some clothing, and the old gentleman purchased me a pair of boots.

I found that I was about fifty or sixty miles from Dayton, in the State of Ohio, and between one and two hundred miles from Cleaveland, on Lake Erie, a place I was desirous of reaching on my way to Canada. This I know will sound strangely to the ears of people in foreign lands, but it is nevertheless true. An American citizen was fleeing from a democratic, republican, Christian government, to receive protection under the monarchy of Great Britain. While the people of the United States boast of their freedom, they at the same time keep three millions of their own citizens in chains; and while I am seated here in sight of Bunker Hill Monument, writing this narrative, I am a slave, and no law, not even in Massachusetts, can protect me from the hands of the slave-holder!

Before leaving this good Quaker friend, he inquired what my name was besides William. I told him that I had no other name. "Well," said he, "thee must have another name. Since thee has got out of slavery, thee has become a man, and men always have two names."

I told him that he was the first man to extend the hand of friendship to me, and I would give him the privilege of naming me.

"If I name thee," said he, "I shall call thee Wells Brown, after myself."

---

*A search for more information about Wells Brown by Professor W. Edward Farrison yielded no results. See W. Edward Farrison, "A Flight Across Ohio: The Escape of William Wells Brown From Slavery," *Ohio State Archaeological and Historical Quarterly,* 61:280 (July, 1952).

"But," said I, "I am not willing to lose my name of William. As it was taken from me once against my will, I am not willing to part with it again upon any terms.

"Then," said he, "I will call thee William Wells Brown."

"So be it," said I; and I have been known by that name ever since I left the house of my first white friend, Wells Brown.

After giving me some little change, I again started for Canada. In four days I reached a public house, and went in to warm myself. I there learned that some fugitive slaves had just passed through the place. The men in the bar-room were talking about it, and I thought that it must have been myself they referred to, and I was therefore afraid to start, fearing they would seize me; but I finally mustered courage enough, and took my leave. As soon as I was out of sight, I went into the woods, and remained there until night, when I again regained the road, and travelled on until next day.

Not having had any food for nearly two days, I was faint with hunger, and was in a dilemma what to do, as the little cash supplied me by my adopted father, and which had contributed to my comfort, was now all gone. I however concluded to go to a farm-house, and ask for something to eat. On approaching the door of the first one presenting itself, I knocked, and was soon met by a man who asked me what I wanted. I told him that I would like something to eat. He asked me where I was from, and where I was going. I replied that I had come some way, and was going to Cleaveland.

After hesitating a moment or two, he told me that he could give me nothing to eat, adding, "that if I would work, I could get something to eat."

I felt bad, being thus refused something to sustain nature, but did not dare tell him that I was a slave.

Just as I was leaving the door, with a heavy heart, a woman, who proved to be the wife of this gentleman, came to the door, and asked her husband what I wanted. He did not seem inclined to inform her. She therefore asked me herself. I told her that I had asked for something to eat. After a few other questions, she told me to come in, and that she would give me something to eat.

I walked up to the door, but the husband remained in the passage, as if unwilling to let me enter.

She asked him two or three times to get out of the way, and let me in. But as he did not move, she pushed him on one side, bidding me walk in! I was never before so glad to see a woman push a man aside! Ever since that act, I have been in favor of "woman's rights!"

After giving me as much food as I could eat, she presented me with ten cents, all the money then at her disposal, accompanied with a note to a friend, a few miles further on the road. Thanking this angel of mercy from an overflowing heart, I pushed on my way, and in three days arrived at Cleaveland, Ohio.

Being an entire stranger in this place, it was difficult for me to find where to stop. I had no money, and the lake being frozen, I saw that I must remain until the opening of the navigation, or go to Canada by way of Buffalo. But believing myself to be somewhat out of danger, I secured an engagement at the Mansion House, as a table waiter, in payment for my board. The proprietor, however, whose name was E. M. Segur, in a short time, hired me for twelve dollars a month; on which terms I remained until spring, when I found good employment on board a lake steamboat.

I purchased some books, and at leisure moments perused them with considerable advantage to myself. While at Cleaveland, I saw, for the first time, an anti-slavery newspaper. It was the *"Genius of Universal Emancipation,"* published by Benjamin Lundy; and though I had no home, I subscribed for the paper. It was my great desire, being out of slavery myself, to do what I could for the emancipation of my brethren yet in chains, and while on Lake Erie, I found many opportunities of "helping their cause along."

It is well known that a great number of fugitives make their escape to Canada, by way of Cleaveland; and while on the lakes, I always made arrangement to carry them on the boat to Buffalo or Detroit, and thus effect their escape to the "promised land." The friends of the slave, knowing that I would transport them without charge, never failed to have a delegation when the boat arrived at Cleaveland. I have sometimes had four or five on board at one time.

In the year 1842, I conveyed, from the first of May to the first of December, sixty-nine fugitives over Lake Erie to Canada. In 1843, I visited Malden, in Upper Canada, and counted seventeen in that small village, whom I had assisted in reaching Canada. Soon after coming north I subscribed for the Liberator, edited by that champion of freedom, William Lloyd Garrison. I had heard nothing of the anti-slavery movement while in slavery, and as soon as I found that my enslaved countrymen had friends who were laboring for their liberation, I felt anxious to join them, and give what aid I could to the cause.

I early embraced the temperance cause, and found that a temperance reformation was needed among my colored brethren. In company with a few friends, I commenced a temperance reformation among the colored people in the city of Buffalo, and labored three years, in which time a society was built up, numbering over five hundred out of a population of less than seven hundred.

In the autumn, 1843, impressed with the importance of spreading anti-slavery truth, as a means to bring about the abolition of slavery, I commenced lecturing as an agent of the western New York Anti-Slavery Society, and have ever since devoted my time to the cause of my enslaved countrymen.

From the Liberty Bell of 1848*

THE AMERICAN SLAVE-TRADE

BY WILLIAMS WELLS BROWN

Of the many features which American slavery presents, the most cruel is that of the slave-trade. A traffic in the bodies and souls of native-born Americans is carried on in the slave-holding states to an extent little dreamed of by the great mass of the people in the non-slave-holding states. The precise number of slaves carried from the slave-raising to the slave-consuming states we have no means of knowing. But it must be very great, as forty thousand were sold and carried out of the State of Virginia in one single year!

This heart-rending and cruel traffic is not confined to any particular class of persons. No person forfeits his or her character or standing in society by being engaged in raising and selling slaves to supply the cotton, sugar, and rice plantations of the south. Few persons who have visited the slave states have not, on their return, told of the gangs of slaves they had seen on their way to the southern market. This trade presents some of the most revolting and atrocious scenes which can be imagined. Slave-prisons, slave-auctions, hand-cuffs, whips, chains, bloodhounds, and other instruments of cruelty, are part of the furniture which belongs to the American slave-trade. It is enough to make humanity bleed at every pore, to see these implements of torture.

Known to God only is the amount of human agony and suffering which sends its cry from these slave-prisons, unheard or unheeded by man, up to His ear; mothers weeping for their children—breaking the night-silence with the shrieks of their breaking hearts. We wish no

---

*The Liberty Bell, edited by Maria Weston Chapman, was an anti-slavery annual published irregularly from 1839 to 1858 as a gift book to raise money for the cause.

human being to experience emotions of needless pain, but we do wish that every man, woman, and child in New England, could visit a southern slave-prison and auction-stand.

I shall never forget a scene which took place in the city of St. Louis, while I was in slavery. A man and his wife, both slaves, were brought from the country to the city, for sale. They were taken to the rooms of Austin & Savage, auctioneers. Several slave-speculators, who are always to be found at auctions where slaves are to be sold, were present. The man was first put up, and sold to the highest bidder. The wife was next ordered to ascend the platform. I was present. She slowly obeyed the order. The auctioneer commenced, and soon several hundred dollars were bid. My eyes were intensely fixed on the face of the woman, whose cheeks were wet with tears. But a conversation between the slave and his new master attracted my attention. I drew near them to listen. The slave was begging his new master to purchase his wife. Said he, "Master, if you will only buy Fanny, I know you will get the worth of your money. She is a good cook, a good washer, and her last mistress liked her very much. If you will only buy her how happy I shall be." The new master replied that he did not want her, but if she sold cheap he would purchase her. I watched the countenance of the man while the different persons were bidding on his wife. When his new master bid on his wife you could see the smile upon his countenance, and the tears stop; but as soon as another would bid, you could see the countenance change and the tears start afresh. From this change of countenance one could see the workings of the inmost soul. But this suspense did not last long; the wife was struck off to the highest bidder, who proved not to be the owner of her husband. As soon as they became aware that they were to be separated, they both burst into tears; and as she descended from the auction-stand, the husband, walking up to her and taking her by the hand, said, "Well, Fanny, we are to part forever, on earth; you have been a good wife to me. I did all that I could to get my new master to buy you; but he did not want you, and all I have to say is, I hope you will try to meet me in heaven. I shall try to meet you there." The wife made no reply, but her sobs and cries told, too well, her own feelings. I saw the countenances of a number of whites who were present, and whose eyes were dim with tears at hearing the man bid his wife farewell.

Such are but common occurrences in the slave states. At these auction-stands, bones, muscles, sinews, blood and nerves, of human beings, are sold with as much indifference as a farmer in the north sells a horse or sheep. And this great American nation is, at the present time, engaged in the slave-trade. I have before me now the Washington "Union," the organ of the government, in which I find an advertisement of several slaves to be sold for the benefit of the government. They will, in all human probability, find homes among the rice-swamps of Georgia, or the cane-brakes of Mississippi.

With every disposition on the part of those who are engaged in it to veil the truth, certain facts have, from time to time, transpired, sufficient to show, if not the full amount of the evil, at least that it is one of prodigious magnitude. And what is more to be wondered at, is the fact that the greatest slave-market is to be found at the capital of the country! The American slave-trader marches by the capitol with his "coffle-gang,"—the stars and stripes waving over their heads, and the constitution of the United States in his pocket.!

The Alexandria Gazette, speaking of the slave-trade at the capital, says, "Here you may behold fathers and brothers leaving behind them the dearest objects of affection, and moving slowly along in the mute agony of despair; there, the young mother, sobbing over the infant whose innocent smile seems but to increase her misery. From some you will hear the burst of bitter lamentation, while from others, the loud hysteric laugh breaks forth, denoting still deeper agony. Such is but a faint picture of the American slave-trade."

Boston, Massachusetts.

THE BLIND SLAVE BOY

BY MRS. BAILEY *

Come back to me mother! why linger away
From thy poor little blind boy the long weary day!
I mark every footstep, I list to each tone,
And wonder my mother should leave me alone!

---

*Mrs. Gamaliel Bailey, whose husband was editor of the *National Era,* an antislavery newspaper published in Washington, D.C.

There are voices of sorrow, and voices of glee,
But there's no one to joy or to sorrow with me;
For each hath of pleasure and trouble his share,
And none for the poor little blind boy will care.

My mother, come back to me! close to thy breast
Once more let thy poor little blind boy be pressed;
Once more let me feel thy warm breath on my cheek,
And hear thee in accents of tenderness speak.
O mother! I've no one to love me—no heart
Can bear like thine own in my sorrows a part,
No hand is so gentle, no voice is so kind,
Oh! none like a mother can cherish the blind!

Poor blind one! No mother thy wailing can hear,
No mother can hasten to banish thy fear;
For the slave-owner drives her o'er mountain and wild,
And for one paltry dollar hath sold thee, poor child;
Ah, who can in language of mortals reveal
The anguish that none but a mother can feel.
When man in his vile lust of mammon hath trod
On her child, who is stricken or smitten of God!

Blind, helpless, forsaken, with strangers alone,
She hears in her anguish his piteous moan;
As he eagerly listens—but listens in vain—
To catch the loved tones of his mother again!
The curse of the broken in spirit shall fall
On the wretch who hath mingled this wormwood and gall,
And his gain like a mildew shall blight and destroy,
Who hath torn from his mother the little blind boy!

APPENDIX

In giving a history of my own sufferings in slavery, as well as the sufferings of others with which I was acquainted, or which came under my immediate observation, I have spoken harshly of slave-holders, in church and state.

Nor am I inclined to apologize for anything which I have said. There are exceptions among slaveholders, as well as among other sinners; and the fact that a slaveholder feeds his slaves better, clothes them better, than another, does not alter the case; he is a slaveholder. I do not ask the slaveholder to feed, clothe, or to treat his victim better as a slave. I am not waging a warfare against the collateral evils, or what are sometimes called the abuses, of slavery. I wage a war against slavery itself, because it takes man down from the lofty position which God intended he should occupy, and places him upon a level with the beasts of the field. It decrees that the slave shall not worship God according to the dictates of his own conscience; it denies him the word of God; it makes him a chattel, and sells him in the market to the highest bidder; it decrees that he shall not protect the wife of his bosom; it takes from him every right which God gave him. Clothing and food are as nothing compared with liberty. What care I for clothing or food, while I am the slave of another? You may take me and put cloth upon my back, boots upon my feet, a hat upon my head, and cram a beef-steak down my throat, and all of this will not satisfy me as long as I know that you have the power to tear me from my dearest relatives. All I ask of the slaveholder is to give the slave his liberty. It is freedom I ask for the *slave*. And that the American slave will eventually get his freedom, no one can doubt. You cannot keep the human mind forever locked up in darkness. A

54

ray of light, a spark from freedom's altar, the idea of inherent right, each, all, will become fixed in the soul; and that moment his "limbs swell beyond the measure of his chains," that moment he is free; then it is that the slave dies to become a freeman; then it is felt that one hour of virtuous liberty is worth an eternity of bondage; then it is, in the madness and fury of his blood, that the excited soul exclaims,

> "From life without freedom, oh! who would not fly;
> For one day of freedom, oh! who would not die?"

The rising of the slaves in Southampton, Virginia, in 1831, has not been forgotten by the American people. Nat Turner, a slave for life,—a Baptist minister,—entertained the idea that he was another Moses, whose duty it was to lead his people out of bondage. His soul was fired with the love of liberty, and he declared to his fellow-slaves that the time had arrived, and that "They who would be free, themselves must strike the blow." He knew that it would be "liberty or death" with his little band of patriots, numbering less than three hundred. He commenced the struggle for liberty; he knew his cause was just, and he loved liberty more than he feared death. He did not wish to take the lives of the whites; he only demanded that himself and brethren might be free. The slaveholders found that men whose souls were burning for liberty, however small their numbers, could not be put down at their pleasure; that something more than water was wanted to extinguish the flame. They trembled at the idea of meeting men in open combat, whose backs they had lacerated, whose wives and daughters they had torn from their bosoms, whose hearts were bleeding from the wounds inflicted by them. They appealed to the United States government for assistance. A company of United States troops was sent into Virginia to put down men whose only offence was, that they wanted to be free. Yes! northern men, men born and brought up in the free states, at the demand of slavery, marched to its rescue. They succeeded in reducing the poor slave again to his chains; but they did not succeed in crushing his spirit.

Not the combined powers of the American Union, not the slaveholders, with all their northern allies, can extinguish that burning desire of freedom in the slave's soul! Northern men may stand by as the body-guard of slaveholders. They may succeed for the time being in keeping the slave in his chains; but unless the slaveholders liberate their victims, and that, too, speedily, some modern Hannibal will make his appearance in the southern states, who will trouble the slaveholders as the noble Carthaginian did the Romans. Abolitionists deprecate the shedding of blood; they have warned the slaveholders again and again. Yet they will not give heed, but still persist in robbing the slave of liberty.

"But for the fear of northern bayonets, pledged for the master's protection, the slaves would long since have wrung a peaceful emancipation from the fears of their oppressors, or sealed their own redemption in blood." To the shame of the northern people, the slaveholders confess that to them they are "indebted for a permanent safe-guard against insurrection;" that "a million of their slaves stand ready to strike for liberty at the first tap of the drum;" and but for the aid of the north they would be too weak to keep them in their chains. I ask in the language of the slave's poet,

> "What! shall ye guard your neighbor still,
> While woman shrieks beneath his rod,
> And while he tramples down at will
> The image of a common God?
> Shall watch and ward be 'round him set,
> Of northern nerve and bayonet?"

The countenance of the people at the north has quieted the fears of the slaveholders, especially the countenance which they receive from northern churches. "But for the countenance of the northern church, the southern conscience would have long since awakened to its guilt: and the impious sight of a church made up of slaveholders, and called the church of Christ, been scouted from the world." So says a distinguished writer.

Slaveholders hide themselves behind the church. A more praying, preaching, psalm-singing people cannot be found than the slave-holders at the south. The religion of the south is referred to every day, to prove that slaveholders are good, pious men. But with all their pretensions, and all the aid which they get from the northern church, they cannot succeed in deceiving the Christian portion of the world. Their child-robbing, man-stealing, woman-whipping, chain-forging, marriage-destroying, slave-manufacturing, man-slaying religion, will not be received as genuine; and the people of the free states cannot expect to live in union with slaveholders, without becoming contaminated with slavery. They are looked upon as one people; they *are* one people; the people in the free and slave states form the "American Union." Slavery is a national institution. The nation licenses men to traffic in the bodies and souls of men; it supplies them with public buildings at the capital of the country to keep their victims in. For a paltry sum it gives the auctioneer a license to sell American men, women, and children, upon the auction-stand. The American slave-trader, with the constitution in his hat and his license in his pocket, marches his gang of chained men and women under the very eaves of the nation's capitol. And this, too, in a country professing to be the freest nation in the world. They profess to be democrats, republicans, and to believe in the natural equality of men; that they are "all created with certain inalienable rights, among which are life, liberty, and the pursuit of happiness." They call themselves a Christian nation; they rob three millions of their countrymen of their liberties, and then talk of their piety, their democracy and their love of liberty; and in the language of Shakspeare, say,

> "And thus I clothe my naked villany,
> And seem a saint when most I play the devil."

The people of the United States, with all their high professions, are forging chains for unborn millions, in their wars for slavery. With all their democracy, there is not a foot of land over which the "stars and stripes" fly, upon which the American slave can stand and claim protection. Whenever the United States constitution has jurisdiction, and the American flag is seen flying, they point out the slave as a chattel, a thing, a piece of property. But I thank God there is one spot in America upon which the slave can stand and be a man. No matter whether the claimant be a United States president, or a doctor of divinity; no matter with what solemnities some American court may have pronounced him a slave; the moment he makes his escape from under the "stars and stripes," and sets foot upon the soil of CANADA, "the altar and the god sink together in the dust; his soul walks abroad in his own majesty; his body swells beyond the measure of his chains, that burst from around him; and he stands redeemed, regenerated, and disenthralled, by the irresistible genius of universal emancipation."

But slavery must and will be banished from the United States soil:

"Let tyrants scorn, while tyrants dare,
The shrieks and writhings of despair;
The end will come, it will not wait,
Bonds, yokes, and scourges have their date;
Slavery itself must pass away,
And be a tale of yesterday."

But I will now stop, and let the slaveholders speak for themselves. I shall here present some evidences of the treatment which slaves receive from their masters; after which I will present a few of the slave-laws. And it has been said, and I believe truly, that no people were ever found to be better than their laws. And, as an American slave,—as one who is identified with the slaves of the south by the scars which I carry on my back,—as one identified with them by the tenderest ties of nature,—as one whose highest aspirations are to serve the cause of truth and freedom,—I beg of the reader not to lay this book down until he or she has read every page it contains. I ask it not for my own sake, but for the sake of three millions who cannot speak for themselves.

From the Livingston County (Albama) Whig of Nov. 16, 1845

"Negro Dogs.—The undersigned having bought the entire pack of Negro Dogs, (of the Hays & Allen stock,) he now proposes to catch runaway Negroes. His charge will be three dollars per day for hunting, and fifteen dollars for catching a runaway. He resides three and a half miles north of Livingston, near the lower Jones' Bluff road.

"William Gambrel.
"Nov. 6, 1845."

The Wilmington [North Carolina] Advertiser of July 13, 1838, contains the following advertisement:

"Ranaway, my Negro man Richard. A reward of $25 will be paid for his apprehension, DEAD or ALIVE. Satisfactory proof will only be required of his being killed. He has with him, in all probability, his wife Eliza, who ran away from Col. Thompson, now a resident of Alabama, about the time he commenced his journey to that state.

"D.H. Rhodes."

The St. Louis Gazette says—

"A wealthy man here had a boy named Reuben, almost white, whom he caused to be branded in the face with the words 'A slave for life.' "

From the N. C. Standard, July 28, 1838.

"Twenty Dollars Reward.—Ranaway from the subscriber, a negro woman and two children; the woman is tall and black, and *a few days before she went off* I burnt her on the left side of her face: I tried to make the letter M, *and she kept a cloth over her head and face, and a fly bonnet over her head, so as to cover the burn;* her children are both boys, the oldest is in his seventh year; he is a *mulatto* and has blue eyes; the youngest is a black, and is in his fifth year.

"Micajah Ricks, Nash County."

"One of my neighbors sold to a speculator a negro boy, about 14 years old. It was more than his poor mother could bear. Her reason fled, and she became a perfect *maniac,* and had to be kept in close confinement. She would occasionally get out and run off to the neighbors. On one of these occasions she came to my house. With tears rolling down her cheeks, and her frame shaking with agony, she would cry out, *'Don't you hear him—they are whipping him now, and he is calling for me!'* This neighbor of mine, who tore the boy away from his poor mother, and thus broke her heart, was a *member of the Presbyterian church.''—Rev. Francis Hawley, Baptist minister, Colebrook, Ct.*

A colored man in the city of St. Louis was taken by a mob, and burnt alive at the stake. A bystander gives the following account of the scene:—

"After the flames had surrounded their prey, and when his clothes were in a blaze all over him, his eyes burnt out of his head, and his mouth seemingly parched to a cinder, some one in the *crowd,* more compassionate then the rest, proposed to put an end to his misery by shooting him, when it was replied, that it would be of no use, since he was already out of his pain. 'No,' said the wretch, 'I am not, I am suffering as much as ever,—shoot me, shoot me.' 'No, no,' said one of the fiends, who was standing about the sacrifice they were roasting, 'he shall not be shot; I would sooner slacken the fire, if that would increase his misery;' and the man who said this was, we understand, an *officer of justice.*"—*Alton Telegraph.*

"We have been informed that the slave William, who murdered his master (Huskey) some weeks since, was taken by a party a few days since from the sheriff of Hot Spring, and *burned alive!* yes, tied up to the limb of a tree and a fire built under him, and consumed in a slow lingering torture."—*Arkansas Gazette,* Oct. 29, 1836.

The Natchez Free Trader, 16th June, 1842, gives a horrible account of the execution of the negro Joseph on the 5th of that month for murder.

"The body," says the paper, "was taken and chained to a tree immediately on the bank of the Mississippi, on what is called Union Point. The torches were lighted and placed in the pile. He watched unmoved the curling flame as it grew, until it began to entwine itself around and feed upon his body; then he sent forth cries of agony painful to the ear, begging some one to blow his brains out; at the same time surging with almost superhuman strength, until the staple with which the chain was fastened to the tree, not being well secured, drew out, and he leaped from the burning pile. At that moment the sharp ring of several rifles was heard, and the body of the negro fell a corpse to the ground. He was picked up by two or three, and again thrown into the fire and consumed."

"Another Negro burned.— We learn from the clerk of the Highlander, that, while wooding a short distance below the mouth of Red river, they were *invited to stop a short time and see another negro burned.*"—*New Orleans Bulletin.*

We can assure the Bostonians, one and all, who have embarked in the nefarious scheme of abolishing slavery at the south, that lashes will hereafter be spared the backs of their emissaries. Let them send out their men to Louisiana; they will never return to tell their sufferings, but they shall expiate the crime of interfering in our domestic institutions by being burned at the stake."—*New Orleans True American.*

"The cry of the whole south should be death, instant death, to the abolitionist, wherever he is caught."—*Augusta (Geo.) Chronicle.*

"Let us declare through the public journals of our country, that the question of slavery is not and shall not be open for discussion: that the system is too deep-rooted among us, and must remain forever; that the very moment any private individual attempts to lecture us upon its evils and immorality, and the necessity of putting means in operation to secure us from them, in the same moment his tongue shall be cut out and cast upon the dunghill."—*Columbia (S. C.) Telescope.*

From the St. Louis Republican.

"On Friday last the coroner held an inquest at the house of Judge Dunica, a few miles south of the city, over the body of a negro girl, about 8 years of age, belonging to Mr. Cordell. The body exhibited evidence of the most cruel whipping and beating we have ever heard of. The flesh on the back and limbs were beaten to a jelly—one shoulder-bone was laid bare—there were several cuts, apparently from a club, on the head—and around the neck was the indentation of a cord, by which it is supposed she had been confined to a tree. She had been hired by a man by the name of Tanner, residing in the neighborhood, and was sent home in this condition. After coming home, her constant request, until her death, was for bread, by which it would seem that she had been starved as well as unmercifully whipped. The jury returned a verdict that she came to her death by the blows inflicted by some persons unknown whilst she was in the employ of Mr. Tanner. Mrs. Tanner has been tried and acquitted."

A correspondent of the N. Y. Herald writes from St. Louis, Oct. 19:

"I yesterday visited the cell of Cornelia, the slave charged with being the accomplice of Mrs. Ann Tanner (recently acquitted) in the murder of a little negro girl, by whipping and starvation. She admits her participancy, but says she was compelled to take the part she did in the affair. On one occasion she says the child was tied to a tree from Monday morning till Friday night, exposed by day to the scorching rays of the sun, and by night to the stinging of myriads of musquitoes; and that during all this time the child had nothing to eat, but was whipped daily. The child told the same story to Dr. McDowell."

From the Carroll County Mississippian, May 4th, 1844.

"Committed to jail in this place, on the 29th of April last, a runaway slave named Creesy, and says she belongs to William Barrow, of Carroll county, Mississippi. Said woman is stout built, five feet four inches high, and appears to be about twenty years of age; she has a band of iron on each ankle, and a trace chain around her neck, fastened with a common padlock.

"J. N. Spencer, Jailer.

"May 15, 1844."

The Savannah, Ga., Republican of the 13th of March, 1845, contains an advertisement, one item of which is as follows:—

"Also, at the same time and place, the following negro slaves, to wit: Charles, Peggy, Antonnett, Davy, September, Maria, Jenny, and Isaac—levied on as the property of Henry T. Hall, to satisfy a mortgage fi. fia. issued out of McIntosh Superior Court, in favor of the board of directors of the *Theological Seminary of the Synod of South Carolina and Georgia,* vs. said Henry T. Hall. Conditions, cash.

"C. O'Neal, Deputy Sheriff, M.C."

In the "Macon (Georgia) Telegraph," May 28, is the following:

"About the first of March last, the negro man Ransom left me, without the least provocation whatever. I will give a reward of $20 dollars for said negro, if taken dead or alive,—and if killed in any attempt an advance of $5 will be paid.

"Bryant Johnson.

"Crawford Co., Ga."

From the Apalachicola Gazette, May 9.

"One Hundred and Fifty Dollars Reward.—Ranaway from my plantation on the 6th inst., three negro men, all of dark complexion.

Bill is about five feet four inches high, aged about twenty-six, *a scar on his upper lip,* also *one on his shoulder,* and has been *badly cut on his arm;* speaks quick and broken, and a venomous look.

"Daniel is about the same height, chunky and well set, broad, flat mouth, with a pleasing countenance, rather inclined to show his teeth when talking, no particular marks recollected, aged about twenty-three.

"Noah is about six feet three or four inches high, twenty-eight years old, with rather a down, impudent look, insolent in his discourse, with a large mark on his breast, *a good many large scars,* caused by the whip, on his back—*has been shot in the back of his arm* with small shot. The above reward will be paid to any one who will kill the three, or fifty for each one, or twenty dollars apiece for them delivered to me at my plantation alive, on Chattahoochie, Early county.

"J. McDonald."

From the Alabama Beacon, June 14, 1845.

"Ranaway, on the 15th of May, from me, a negro woman named Fanny. Said woman is twenty years old; is rather tall, can read and write, and so forge passes for herself. Carried away with her a pair of ear-rings, a Bible with a red cover, is very pious. She prays a great deal, and was, as supposed, contented and happy. She is as white as most white women, with straight light hair, and blue eyes, and can pass herself for a white woman. I will give five hundred dollars for her apprehension and delivery to me. She is very intelligent.

"Tuscaloosa, May, 29, 1845."   "John Balch.

From the N. O. Commercial Bulletin, Sept. 30.

"Ten Dollars Reward.—Ranaway from the subscribers, on the 15th of last month, the negro man Charles, about 45 years of age, 5 feet 6 inches high; red complexion, has had the *upper lid of his right eye torn, and a scar on his forehead;* speaks English only, and stutters when spoken to; he had on when he left, *an iron collar, the prongs of which he broke off before absconding.* The above reward will be paid for the arrest of said slave.   W. E. & R. Murphy,

"132 Old Raisin."

From the N. O. Bee, Oct. 5.

"Ranaway from the residence of Messrs. F. Duncom & Co., the negro Francois, aged from 25 to 30 years, about 5 feet 1 inch in height; the *upper front teeth are missing;* he had *chains on both of his legs,* dressed with a kind of blouse made of sackcloth. A proportionate reward will be given to whoever will bring him back to the bakery, No. 74, Bourbon street."

From the N. O. Picayune of Sunday, Dec. 17.

"Cock-Pit.—*Benefit of Fire Company No.* 1,   *Lafayette.* —A cock-fight will take place on Sunday, the 17th inst., at the well-known house of the subscriber. As the entire proceeds are for the benefit of the fire company, a full attendance is respectfully solicited.

"Corner of Josephine and Tchoupitolas streets, Lafayette."

From the N. O. Picayune.

"Turkey Shooting.—This day, Dec. 17, from 10 o'clock, A. M., until 6 o'clock, P. M., and the following Sundays at M'Donoughville, opposite the Second Municipality Ferry."

The next is an advertisement from the New Orleans Bee, an equally popular paper.

"A Bull Fight, between a ferocious bull and a number of dogs, will take place on Sunday next, at 4¼ o'clock, P. M., on the other side of the river, at Algiers, opposite Canal street. After the bull fight, a fight will take place between a bear and some dogs. The whole to conclude by a combat between an ass and several dogs.

"Amateurs bringing dogs to participate in the fight will be admitted gratis. Admittance—Boxes, 50 cts.; Pit, 30 cts. The spectacle will be repeated every Sunday, weather permitting.

"Pepe Llulla."

EXTRACTS FROM THE AMERICAN SLAVE CODE.

The following are mostly abridged selections from the statutes of the slave states and of the United States. They give but a faint view of the cruel oppression to which the slaves are subject, but a strong one enough, it is thought, to fill every honest heart with a deep abhorrence of the atrocious system. Most of the important provisions here cited, though placed under the name of only one state, prevail in nearly all the states, with slight variations in language, and some diversity in the penalties. The extracts have been made in part from Stroud's Sketch of the Slave Laws,* but chiefly from authorized editions of the statute books referred to, found in the Philadelphia Law Library. As the compiler has not had access to many of the later enactments of the several states, nearly all he has cited are acts of an earlier date than that of the present anti-slavery movement, so that their severity cannot be ascribed to its influence.

The cardinal principal of slavery, that the slave is not to be ranked among *sentient beings,* but among things—is an article of property, a chattel personal—obtains as undoubted law in all the slave states.[†] —*Stroud's Sketch,* p. 22.

The dominion of the master is as unlimited as is that which is tolerated by the laws of any civilized country in relation to brute animals— to *quadrupeds;* to use the words of the civil law.—*Ib.* 24.

Slaves cannot even contract matrimony.[‡]—*Ib.* 61.

LOUISIANA.—A slave is one who is in the power of his master, to whom he belongs. The master may sell him, dispose of his person, his industry and his labor; he can do nothing, possess nothing, nor acquire anything, but what must belong to his master.—*Civil Code,* Art. 35.

Slaves are incapable of inheriting or transmitting property.—*Civil Code,* Art. 945; also Art. 175, and *Code of Practice,* Art. 103.

Martin's Digest, Act of June 7, 1806.—Slaves shall always be reputed and considered real estate; shall be as such subject to be mortgaged, according to the rules prescribed by law, and they shall be seized and sold as real estate.—*Vol. I.,* p. 612.

---

*George McDowell Stroud, *A Sketch of the Laws Relating to Slavery in the Several States of the United States of America* (Philadelphia, 1827).

[†]In accourdance with this doctrine, an act of Maryland, 1798, enumerates among articles of property, *"slaves, working beasts, animals of any kind, stock, furniture, plate, and so forth."—Ib* 23.

[‡]A slave is not admonished for incontinence, punished for adultery, nor prosecuted for bigamy.—*Attorney General of Maryland, Md. Rep. Vol I.* 561.

Dig. Stat. Sec 13—No owner of slaves shall hire his slaves to themselves, under a penalty of twenty-five dollars for each offence. —*Vol. 1.,* p. 102.

Sec. 15.—No slave can possess anything in his own right, or dispose of the produce of his own industry, without the consent of his master.—p. 103.

Sec. 16.—No slave can be party in a civil suit, or witness in a civil or criminal matter, against any white person.—p. 103. *See also Civil Code,* Art. 117, p. 28.

Sec. 18.—A slave's subordination to his master is susceptible of no restriction, (except in what incites to crime,) and he owes to him and all his family, respect without bounds, and absolute obedience.—p. 103.

Sec. 25.—Every slave found on horseback, without a written permission from his master, shall receive twenty-five lashes.—p. 105.

Sec. 32.—Any freeholder may seize and correct any slave found absent from his usual place of work or residence, without some white person, and if the slave resist or try to escape, he may use arms, and if the slave *assult** and strike him, he may *kill* the slave.—p. 109. —p. 115.

Sec. 35.—It is lawful to fire upon runaway negroes who are armed, and upon those who, when pursued, refuse to surrender.—p. 109.

Sec. 38.—No slave may buy, sell, or exchange any kind of goods, or hold any boat, or bring up for his own use any horses or cattle, under a penalty of forfeiting the whole.—p. 110.

Sec. 7.—Slaves or free colored persons are punished with *death* for wilfully burning or destroying any stack of produce or any building.

Sec. 15.—The punishment of a slave for striking a white person, shall be for the first and second offences at the discretion of the court,[†] but not extending to life or limb, and for the third offence *death;* but for grievously wounding or multilating a white person, *death* for the first offence; provided, if the blow or wound is given in

---

*The legal meaning of assult is to *offer* to do personal violence.

[†] A court for the trial of slaves consists of one justice of the peace, and three freeholders, and the justice and one freeholder, i.e., *one half the court, may convict, though the other two are for acquittal.*—*Martin's Dig., I.* 646.

defence of the person or *property of his master,* or the person having charge of him, he is entirely justified.

Act of Feb. 22, 1824, Sec. 2.—A slave for wilfully striking his master or mistress, or the child of either, or his white overseer, so as to cause a bruise or shedding of blood, *shall be punished with death.*—p. 125.

Act of March 6, 1819.—Any person cutting or breaking any iron chain or collar used to prevent the escape of slaves, shall be fined not less than two hundred dollars, nor more than one thousand dollars, and be imprisoned not more than two years nor less than six months.—p. 64 of the session.

Law of January 8, 1813, Sec. 71.—All slaves sentenced to death or perpetual imprisonment, in virtue of existing laws, shall be paid for out of the public treasury, provided the sum paid shall not exceed $300 for each slave.

Law of March 16, 1830, Sec. 93.—The state treasurer shall pay the owners the value of all slaves whose punishment has been commuted from that of death to that of imprisonment for life, &c.

If any slave shall *happen* to be slain for refusing to surrender him or herself, contrary to law, or in unlawfully resisting any officer or *other person,* who shall apprehend, or endeavor to apprehend, such slave or slaves, &c., such officer or *other person so killing such slave as aforesaid,* making resistance, shall be, and he is by this act, *indemnified,* from any prosecution for such killing aforesaid,&c. —*Maryland Laws, act of* 1751, *chap xiv.,*§9.

And by the negro act of 1740 of South Carolina, it is declared:

If any slave who shall be out of the house or plantation where such slave shall live, or shall be usually employed, or without some white person in company with such slave, shall *refuse to submit* to undergo the examination of *any white* person, it shall be lawful for such white person to pursue, apprehend, and moderately correct such slave; and if such slave shall assault and strike such white person, such slave may be *lawfully killed!!*—2 *Brevard's Digest,*231.

MISSISSIPPI. *Chapt.* 92, Sec. 110.—Penalty for any slave or free colored person exercising the functions of a minister of the gospel, thirty-nine lashes; but any master may permit his slave to preach on his own premises, no slaves but his own being permitted to assemble.—*Digest of Stat.,* p. 770.

Act of June 18, 1822, Sec. 21.—No negro or mulatto can be a witness in any case, except against negroes or mulattoes.—p. 749. *New Code,* 372.

Sec. 25.—Any master licensing his slave to go at large and trade as a freeman, shall forfeit fifty dollars to the state for the literary fund.

Penalty for teaching a slave to read, imprisonment one year. For using language having a *tendency* to promote discontent among free colored people, or insubordination among slaves, imprisonment at *hard labor,* not less than three, nor more than twenty-one years, or death, at the discretion of the court.—*L. M. Child's Appeal,* p. 70.

Sec. 26.— It is *lawful* for *any* person, and the duty of every sheriff, deputy-sheriff, coroner and constable to apprehend any slave going at large, or hired out by him, or herself, and take him or her before a justice of the peace, who shall impose a penalty of not less than twenty dollars, nor more than fifty dollars, on the owner, who has permitted such slave to do so.

Sec. 32.—Any negro or mulatto, for using abusive language, or lifting his hand in opposition to any white person, (except in self-defence against a wanton assault,) shall, on proof of the offence by oath of such person, receive such punishment as a justice of the peace may order, not exceeding thirty-nine lashes.

Sec. 41.—Forbids the holding of cattle, sheep or hogs by slaves, even with consent of the master, under penalty of forfeiture, half to the county, and half to the *informer.*

Sec. 42—Forbids a slave keeping a dog, under a penalty of twenty-five stripes; and requires any master who permits it to pay a fine of five dollars, and make good all damages done by such dog.

Sec. 43—Forbids slaves cultivating cotton for his own use, and imposes a fine of fifty dollars on the master or overseer who permits it.

Revised Code.—Every negro or mulatto found in the state, not able to show himself entitled to freedom, may be sold as a slave—p. 389. The owner of any plantation, on which a slave comes without written leave from his master, and not on lawful business, may inflict ten lashes for every such offence.—p. 371.

ALABAMA.—*Aiken's Digest.* Tit. *Slaves, &c.,* Sec. 31.—For *attempting* to teach any free colored person, or slave, to spell, read or write, a fine of not less than two hundred and fifty dollars, nor more than five hundred dollars!—p. 397.

Sec. 35 and 36.—Any free colored person found with slaves in a kitchen, outhouse or negro quarter, without a written permission from the master or overseer of said slaves, and any slave found without such permission with a free negro on his premises, shall receive fifteen lashes for the first offence, and thirty-nine for each subsequent offence; to be inflicted by master, overseer, or member of any patrol company.—p. 397.

Toulmin's Digest.—No slave can be emancipated but by a *special* act of the Legislature.—p. 623.

Act Jan. 1st, 1823—Authorizes an agent to be appointed by the governor of the state, *to sell for the benefit of the state* all persons of color brought into the United States and within the jurisdiction of Alabama, *contrary to the laws of congress prohibiting the slave trade.*—p. 643.

GEORGIA.—*Prince's Digest.* Act Dec. 19,1818.—Penalty for any free person of color (except regularly articled seamen) coming into the state, a fine of one hundred dollars on failure of payment to be sold as a slave.—p. 465.

Penalty for permitting a slave to labor or do business for himself, except on his master's premises, thirty dollars per week.—p. 457.

No slave can be a party to any suit against a white man, except on claim of his freedom, *and every colored person is presumed to be a slave, unless he can prove himself free.*—p. 446.

Act Dec. 13, 1792—Forbids the assembling of negroes under pretence of divine worship, contrary to the act regulating patrols, p. 342. This act provides that any justice of the peace may disperse any assembly of slaves which *may* endanger the peace; and every slave found at such meeting shall receive, *without trial,* twenty-five stripes!—p. 447.

Any person who sees more than seven men slaves without any white person, in a high road, may whip each slave *twenty* lashes.—p. 454.

Any slave who harbors a runaway, may suffer punishment *to any extent,* not affecting life or limb.—p. 452.

SOUTH CAROLINA.—*Brevard's Digest.*—Slaves shall be deemed sold, taken, reputed, and adjudged in law to be *chattels personal* in the hands of their owners and possessors, and their executors, administrators, and assigns, *to all intents, constructions and purposes whatever.*—Vol. ii., p. 229.

Act of 1740, in the preamble, states that "*many* owners of slaves and others that have the management of them do confine them *so closely to hard labor,* that they have *not sufficient time for natural rest,*" and enacts that no slave shall be compelled to labor more than *fifteen* hours in the twenty-four from March 25th to Sept. 25th, or *fourteen* in the twenty-four for the rest of the year. Penalty from £5 to £20.—Vol. ii., p. 243.

[Yet, in several of the slave states, the time of work for *criminals* whose *punishment* is hard labor, is eight hours a day for three months, nine hours for two months, and ten for the rest of the year.]

A slave endeavoring to entice another slave to run away, if provision be prepared for the purpose of aiding or abetting such endeavor, shall suffer *death.*—pp. 233 and 244.

Penalty for cruelly scalding or burning a slave, cutting out his tongue, putting out his eye, or depriving him of any limb, a fine of £100. For beating with a *horse*-whip, cow-skin, switch or small stick, or putting irons on, or imprisoning a slave, *no penalty or prohibition.*—p. 241.

Any person who, not having lawful authority to do so, shall beat a slave, so as to disable him from *working,* shall pay fifteen shillings a day *to the owner,* for the slave's lost time, and the charge of his cure.—pp. 231 and 232.

A slave claiming his freedom may sue for it by some friend who will act as guardian, but if the action be judged groundless, said guardian shall pay *double* costs of suit, and such damages to the owner as the court may decide.—p. 260.

Any assembly of slaves or free colored persons, in a secret or confined place, for mental instruction, (even if white persons *are* present,) is an unlawful meeting, and magistrates must disperse it, breaking doors if necessary, and may inflict *twenty lashes* upon each slave or colored person present.—pp. 254 and 255.

Meetings for religious worship, before sunrise, or after 9 o'clock, P. M., unless a majority are white persons, are forbidden; and magistrates are required to disperse them.—p. 261.

A slave who lets loose any boat from the place where the owner has fastened it, for the first *offence shall receive thirty-nine lashes, and for the second shall have one ear cut off.*—p. 228.

James' Digest.—Penalty for *killing* a slave, on *sudden heat of passion,* or by *undue correction,* a fine of $500 and imprisonment not over six months.—p. 392.

NORTH CAROLINA.—*Haywood's Manual.*—Act of 1798, Sec. 3, enacts, that the killing of a slave shall be punished like that of a free man; *except* in the case of a slave *out-lawed,*[*] or a slave *offering to resist* his master, or a slave *dying under moderate correction.*—p. 530.

Act of 1799.—Any slave set free, except for meritorious services, to be adjudged of by the county court, may be seized by any freeholder, committed to jail, *and sold to the highest bidder.*[†]—p. 525.

Patrols are not liable to the master for punishing his slave, unless their conduct clearly shows malice *against the master.*—*Hawk's Reps.,* vol. i., p. 418.

TENNESSEE.—*Stat. Law,* Chap. 57, Sec. 1.—Penalty on master for hiring to any slave his own time, a fine of not less than one dollar nor more than two dollars a day, *half* to the informer.—p. 679.

Chap. 2, Sec. 102.—No slave can be emancipated but on condition of immediately removing from the state, and the person emancipating shall give bond, in a sum equal to the slave's value, to have him removed.—p. 279.

Laws of 1813. Chap. 35.—In the trial of slaves, the sheriff chooses the court, which must consist of three justices and twelve *slaveholders* to serve as jurors.

ARKANSAS.—*Rev. Stat.,* Sec. 4, requires the patrol to visit all places suspected of unlawful assemblages of slaves; and sec. 5 provides that any slave found at such assembly, or strolling about

---

[*] A slave may be out-lawed when he runs away, conceals himself, and, to sustain life, kills a hog, or any animal of the cattle kind.—*Haywood's Manual,* p. 521.

[†] In South Carolina, *any* person may seize such freed man and keep him as his property.

without a pass, *shall receive* any number of *lashes,* at the discretion of the patrol, not exceeding twenty.—p. 604.

MISSOURI.—*Laws, I.*—Any master may commit to jail, there to remain, at *his pleasure,* any slave who refuses to obey him or his overseer.—p. 309.

Whether a slave claiming freedom may even commence a suit for it, may depend on the decision of a single judge.—*Stroud's Sketch,* p. 78, note which refers to Missouri laws, I., 404.

KENTUCKY.—*Dig. of Stat.,* Act Feb. 8, 1798, Sec. 5.—No colored person may *keep* or *carry* gun, powder, shot, *club* or *other weapon,* on penalty of *thirty-nine lashes,* and forfeiting the weapon, which any person is authorized to take.

VIRGINIA.—*Rev. Code.*—Any emancipated slave remaining in the state more than a year, may be sold by the overseers of the *poor,* for the benefit of the *literary fund!*—Vol. i., p. 436.

Any slave or free colored person found at any school for teaching reading or writing, by day or night, may be whipped, at the discretion of a justice, not exceeding twenty lashes.—p. 424.

Suppl. Rev. Code.—Any white person assembling with slaves, for the *purpose* of teaching them to read or write, shall be fined, not less than 10 dollars, nor more than 100 dollars; or with free colored persons, shall be fined not more than fifty dollars, and imprisoned not more than two months.—p. 245.

By the revised code, *seventy-one* offences are punished with *death* when commited by slaves, and by nothing more than imprisonment when by the whites.—*Stroud's Sketch,* p. 107.

Rev. Code.—In the trial of slaves, the court consists of five justices without juries, even in capital cases.—I., p. 420.

MARYLAND.—*Stat. Law,* Sec. 8.—Any slave, for rambling in the night, or riding horses by day without leave, or running away may be punished by whipping, cropping, or branding in the cheek, or otherwise, not rendering him unfit for labor.—p. 237.

Any slave convicted of petty treason, murder, or *wilful burning of dwelling houses,* may be sentenced *to have the right hand cut off, to be hanged in the usual manner, the head severed from the body, the body divided into four quarters, and the head and quarters set up in the most public place in the country where such fact was committed!!*—p. 190.

Act 1717, Chap. 13, Sec. 5—Provides that any free colored person marrying a slave, becomes a slave for life, except mulattoes born of white women.

DELAWARE.—*Laws.*—More than six men slaves, meeting together, not belonging to one master, unless on lawful business of their owners, may be whipped to the extent of twenty-one lashes each.—p. 104.

UNITED STATES.—*Constitution.*—The chief proslavery provisions of the constitution, as is generally known, are, 1st, that by virtue of which the slave states are represented in congress for three-fifths of their slaves;* 2nd, that requiring the giving up of any runaway slaves to their masters: 3rd, that pledging the physical force of the whole country to suppress insurrections, i.e., attempts to gain freedom by such means as the framers of the instrument themselves used.

Act of Feb. 12, 1793—Provides that any master or his agent may seize any person whom he claims as a "fugitive from service," and take him before a judge of the U.S. court, or magistrate of the city or county where he is taken, and the magistrate, on proof, in support of the claim, to his satisfaction, must give the claimant a certificate authorizing the removal of such fugitive to the state he fled from.[†]

DISTRICT OF COLUMBIA.—The act of congress incorporating Washington city, gives the corporation power to prescribe the terms and conditions on which free negroes and mulattoes may reside in the city. *City Laws,* 6 and 11. By this authority, the city in 1827 enacted that any free colored person coming there to reside, should give the mayor satisfactory evidence of his freedom, and enter into bond with two freehold sureties, in the sum of five hundred dollars, for his good conduct, to be renewed each year for three years; or failing to do so, must leave the city, or be committed to the workhouse, for not more than one year, and if he still refuse to to go, may be again committed for the same period, and so on.—*Ib.* 198.

---

* By the operation of this provision, twelve slaveholding states, whose white population only equals that of New York and Ohio, send to congress 24 senators and 102 representatives, while these two states only send 4 senators and 59 representatives.

† Thus it may be seen that a *man* may be doomed to slavery by an authority not considered sufficient to settle a claim of *twenty dollars.*

Colored persons residing in the city, who cannot prove their title to freedom, shall be imprisoned as absconding slaves.—*Ib.* 198.

Colored persons found without free papers may be arrested as runaway slaves, and after two months' notice, if no claimant appears, must be advertised ten days, and sold to pay their jail fees.*—*Stroud*, 85, note.

The city of Washington grants a license to *trade in slaves,* for profit, as agent, or otherwise, for four hundred dollars.—*City Laws,* p. 249.

Reader, you uphold these laws *while you do nothing for their repeal.* You *can do* much. You can take and read the antislavery journals. They will give you an impartial history of the cause, and arguments with which to convert its enemies. You can countenance and aid those who are laboring for its promotion. You can petition against slavery; you can refuse to vote for slaveholders or pro-slavery men, constitutions and compacts; can abstain from products of slave labor; and can use your social influence to spread right principles and awaken a right feeling. Be as earnest for freedom as its foes are for slavery, and you can diffuse an anti-slavery sentiment through your whole neighborhood, and merit "the blessing of them that are ready to perish."

———

The following is from the old colonial law of North Carolina:

Notice of the commitment of runaways—viz., 1741, c. 24, §29. "An act concerning servants and slaves."

Copy of notice containing a full description of such runaway and his clothing.—The sheriff is to "cause a copy of such notice to be sent to the clerk or reader of each church or chapel within his county, who are hereby required to make publication thereof by setting up the same in some open and convenient place, near the said

———

* The prisons of the district, built with the money of the nation, are used as store-houses of the slaveholder's human merchandize. "From the statement of the keeper of a jail at Washington, it appears that in five years, upwards of 450 colored persons were committed to the national prison in that city, for safekeeping, i.e., until they could be disposed of in the course of the *slave trade,* besides nearly 300 who had been taken up as runaways." —*Miner's Speech in H. Rep.,* 1829.

church or chapel, on every Lord's day, during the space of two months from the date thereof."

1741, c. 24, §45.—"Which proclamation shall be published on a Sabbath day at the door of every church or chapel, or, for want of such, at the place where divine service shall be performed in the said county, by the parish clerk or reader, immediately after divine service; and if any slave or slaves, against whom proclamation hath been thus issued, stay out and do not immediately return home, it shall be lawful for any person or persons whatsoever to kill and destroy such slave or slaves by such way or means as he or she shall think fit, without accusation or impeachment of any crime for the same."

It is well known that slavery makes labor disreputable in the slave states. Laboring men of the north, hear how contemptibly slave-holders speak of you.

Mr. Robert Wickliffe of Kentucky, in a speech published in the Louisville Advertiser, in opposition to those who were averse to the importation of slaves from the states, thus discourseth:

"Gentlemen wanted to drive out the black population that they may obtain white negroes in their place. White negroes have this advantage over black negroes, they can be converted into voters; and the men who live upon the sweat of their brow, and pay them but a dependent and scanty subsistence, can, if able to keep then thousand of them in employment, come up to the polls and change the destiny of the country.

"How improved will be our condition when we have such white negroes as perform the servile labors of Europe, of old England, and he would add now of *New England,* when our body servants and our cart drivers, and our street sweepers, are *white negroes* instead of black. Where will be the independence, the proud spirit, and chivalry of the Kentuckians then?"

We believe the servitude which prevails in the south far preferable to that of the *north,* or in Europe. Slavery will exist in all communities. There is a class which may be nominally free, but they will be virtually *slaves."—Mississippian, July 6th, 1838.*

"Those who depend on their daily labor for their daily subsistence can never enter into political affairs, they never do, never will, never can." —*B. W. Leigh in Virginia Convention,* 1829.

"All society settles down into a classification of capitalists and laborers. The former will *own* the latter, either collectively through the government, or individually in a state of domestic servitude as exists in the southern states of this confederacy. If laborers ever obtain the political power of a country, it is in fact in a state of Revolution. The capitalists north of Mason and Dixon's line have precisely the same interest in the labor of the country that the capitalists of England have in their labor. Hence it is, that they must have a strong federal government (!) *to control* the labor of the nation. But it is precisely the reverse with us. We have already not only a right to the proceeds of our laborers, but we own a *class of laborers* themselves. But let me say to gentlemen who represent the great class of capitalists in the north, beware that you do not drive us into a separate system, for if you do, as certain as the decrees of heaven, you will be compelled to *appeal to the sword to maintain yourselves at home.* It may not come in your day; but your children's children will be covered with the blood of domestic factions, and a *plundering mob contending for power and conquest."* —Mr. *Pickens, of South Carolina, in Congress, 21st Jan., 1836.*

"In the very nature of things there must be classes of persons to discharge all the different offices of society from the highest to the lowest. Some of these offices are regarded as *degraded,* although they must and will be performed. Hence those manifest forms of dependent servitude which produce a sense of superiority in the masters or employers, and of inferiority on the part of the servants. Where these offices are performed by *members of the political community,* a dangerous element is obviously introduced into the body politic. Hence the alarming tendency to violate the rights of property by agrarian legislation which is beginning to be manifest in the older states where universal suffrage *prevails without* domestic slavery.

"In a word, the institution of domestic slavery supersedes the *necessity* of An Order of Nobility and All the Other Appendages of a Hereditary System of Government."—*Gov. M'Duffie's Message to the South Carolina Legislature, 1836.*

"We of the south have cause now, and shall soon have greater, to congratulate ourselves on the existence of a population among us which excludes the populace which in effect rules some of our northern neighbors, and is rapidly gaining strength wherever slavery does not exist—a populace made up of the dregs of Europe, and the most worthless portion of the native population."—*Richmond Whig,* 1837.

"Would you do a benefit to the horse or the ox by giving him a cultivated understanding, a fine feeling! So far as the mere laborer has the pride, the knowledge or the aspiration of a freeman, he is unfitted for his situation. If there are sordid, servile, *laborious* offices to be performed, is it not better that there should be sordid, servile, laborious beings to perform them?

"Odium has been cast upon our legislation on account of its forbidding the elements of education being communicated to slaves. But in truth what injury is done them by this? *He who works during the day with his hands,* does not read in the intervals of leisure for his amusement or the improvement of his mind, or the exception is so very rare as scarcely to need the being provided for."—*Chancellor Harper, of South Carolina.—Southern Lit. Messenger.*

"Our slave population is decidedly preferable, as an orderly and laboring class, to a northern laboring class, that have just learning enough to make them wondrous wise, and make them the most dangerous class to well regulated liberty under the sun."*Richmond (Virginia) Enquirer.*

A

LECTURE

DELIVERED BEFORE THE

FEMALE ANTI-SLAVERY SOCIETY
OF SALEM

AT LYCEUM HALL, Nov. 14, 1847

———

By WILLIAM W. BROWN
A FUGITIVE SLAVE

———

REPORTED BY HENRY M. PARKHURST,
Phonographic reporter, Boston

BOSTON:
MASSACHUSETTS ANTI-SLAVERY SOCIETY,
No. 21 Cornhill
1847

LECTURE

Mr. Chairman, and Ladies and Gentlemen:— In coming before you this evening to speak upon this all-important, this great and commanding subject of freedom, I do not appear without considerable embarrassment; nor am I embarrassed without a cause. I find myself standing before an audience whose opportunities for education may well be said to be without limit. I can scarcely walk through a street in your city, or through a city or a town in New England, but I see your common schools, your high schools, and your colleges. And when I recollect that but a few years since, I was upon a Southern plantation, that I was a Slave, a chattel, a thing, a piece of property,—when I recollect that at the age of twenty-one years I was entirely without education, this, every one will agree, is enough to embarrass me. But I do not come here for the purpose of making a grammatical speech, nor for the purpose of making a speech that shall receive the applause of my hearers. I did not accept the invitation to lecture before this association, with the expectation or the hope that I should be able to present anything new. I accepted the invitation because I felt that I owed a duty to the cause of humanity; I felt that I owed a duty to three millions of my brethren and sisters, with some of whom I am identified by the dearest ties of nature, and with most of whom I am identified by the scars which I carry upon my back. This, and this alone, induced me to accept the invitation to lecture here.

My subject for this evening is Slavery as it is, and its influence upon the morals and character of the American people.

I may try to represent to you Slavery as it is; another may follow me and try to represent the condition of the Slave; we may all represent it as we think it is; and yet we shall all fail to represent the real condition of the Slave. Your fastidiousness would not allow me to do it; and if it would, I, for one, should not be willing to do it;—at least to an audience. Were I about to tell you the evils of Slavery, to represent to you the Slave in his lowest degradation, I should wish to take you, one at a time, and whisper it to you.

Slavery has never been represented; Slavery never can be represented. What is a Slave? A Slave is one that is in the power of an owner. He is a chattel; he is a thing; he is a piece of property. A master can dispose of him, can dispose of his labor, can dispose of his wife, can dispose of his offspring, can dispose of everything that belongs to the Slave, and the Slave shall have no right to speak; he shall have nothing to say. The Slave cannot speak for himself; he cannot speak for his wife, or his children. He is a thing. He is a piece of property in the hands of a master, as much as is the horse that belongs to the individual that may ride him through your streets to-morrow. Where we find one man holding an unlimited power over another, I ask, what can we expect to find his condition? Give one man power *ad infinitum* over another, and he will abuse that power; no matter if there be law; no matter if there be public sentiment in favor of the oppressed.

The system of Slavery, that I, in part, represent here this evening, is a system that strikes at the foundation of society, that strikes at the foundation of civil and political institutions. It is a system that takes man down from that lofty position which his God designed that he should occupy; that drags him down, places him upon a level with the beasts of the field, and there keeps him, that it may rob him of his liberty. Slavery is a system that tears the husband from the wife, and the wife from the husband; that tears the child from the mother, and the sister from the brother; that tears asunder the tenderest ties of nature. Slavery is a system that has its blood-hounds, its chains, its negro-whips, its dungeons, and almost every instrument of cruelty that the human eye can look at; and all this for the purpose of keeping the Slave in subjection; all this for the purpose of obliterating the mind, of crushing the intellect, and of annihilating the soul.

I have read somewhere of an individual named Caspar Hauser, who made his appearance in Germany some time since, and represented that he had made his escape from certain persons who had been trying to obliterate his mind, and to annihilate his intellect. The representation of that single individual raised such an excitement in Germany, that law-makers took it in hand examined it, and made a law covering that particular case and all cases that should occur of that kind; and they denominated it the "murder of the soul." Now, I ask, what is Slavery doing in one half of the States of this Union, at the present time? The souls of three millions of American citizens are being murdered every day, under the blighting influence of American Slavery. Twenty thousand have made their escape from the prison-house; some have taken refuge in the Canadas, and others are lurking behind the stumps in the Slave-States. They are telling their tales, and representing that Slavery is not only trying to murder their souls, but the souls of three million of their countrymen at the present day; and the excitement that one individual raised in monarchical Germany, three millions have failed to raise in democratic, Christian, republican America!

I ask, is not this a system that we should examine! Ought we not to look at it? Ought we not to see what the cause is that keeps the people asleep upon the great subject of American Slavery? When I get to talking about Slavery as it is,—when I think of the three millions that are in chains at the present time, I am carried back to the days when I was a Slave upon a Southern plantation; I am carried back to the time when I saw dear relatives, with whom I am identified by the tenderest ties of nature, abused and ill-treated. I am carried back to the time when I saw hundreds of Slaves driven from the Slave-growing to the Slave-consuming States. When I begin to talk of Slavery, the sighs and the groans of three millions of my countrymen come to me upon the wings of every wind; and it causes me to feel sad, even when I think I am making a successful effort in representing the condition of the Slave.

What is the protection from the masters which Slaves receive? Some say, law; others, public sentiment. But, I ask, Where is the law; where is the public sentiment? If it is there, it is not effectual; it will not protect the Slave. Has the case ever occurred where the Slaveholder has been sent to the State's Prison, or anything of the kind, for ill-treating, or for murdering a Slave? No such case is upon record; and it is because the Slave receives no protection and can expect no protection from the hands of the master. What has the brother not done, upon the Slave-plantation, for the purpose of protecting the chastity of a dearly beloved sister? What has the father not done to protect the chastity of his daughter? What has the husband not done to protect his wife from the hands of the tyrant? They have committed murders. The mother has taken the life of her child, to preserve that child from the hands of the Slave-trader. The brother has taken the life of his sister, to protect her chastity. As the noble Virginius seized the dagger, and thrust it to the heart of the gentle Virginia, to save her from the hands of Appius Claudius of Rome, so has the father seized the deadly knife, and taken the life of his daughter, to save her from the hands of the master or of the Negro-driver. And yet we are told that the Slave is protected; that there is law and public sentiment! It is all a dead letter to the Slave.

But why stand here and try to represent the condition of the Slave? My whole subject must necessarily represent his condition, and I will therefore pass to the second part,—the influence of Slavery upon the morals of the people; not only upon the morals of the Slave-holding South, or of the Slave, but upon the morals of the people of the United States of America. I am not willing to draw a line between the people of the North and the people of the South. So far as the people of the North are connected with Slaveholding, they necessarily become contaminated by the evils that follow in the train of Slavery.

Let me look at the influence which Slavery has over the morals of the people of the South. Three millions of Slaves unprotected! A million of females that have no right to marriage! Among the three millions of Slaves upon the Southern plantations, not a single lawful marriage can be found! They are out of the pale of the law. They are herded together, so far as the law is concerned, as so many beasts of burden are in the free States.

Talk about the influence of Slavery upon the morals of the people, when the Slave is sold in the Slave-holding States for the benefit of the church? when he is sold for the purpose of building churches? when he is sold for the benefit of the minister?

I have before me a few advertisements, taken from public journals and papers, published in the Slaveholding States of this Union. I have one or two that I will read to the audience, for I am satisfied that no

evidence is so effectual for the purpose of convincing the people of
the North of the great evils of Slavery as is the evidence of
Slaveholders themselves. I do not present to you the assertion of the
North; I do not bring before you the advertisement of the
Abolitionists, or my own assertion; but I bring before you the
testimony of the Slaveholders themselves,—and by their own
testimony must they stand or fall.

The first is an advertisement from the columns of the New Orleans
Picayune, one of the most reputable papers published in the State of
Louisiana, and I may say one of the most reputable papers published
South of Mason and Dixon's line. If you take up the Boston Courier,
or any other reputable paper, you will probably find in it an extract
from the New Orleans Picayune, whose editor is at the present time
in Mexico, where our people are cutting the throats of their
neighbors.

"Cock-pit—Benefit of Fire Company No. 1, Lafayette.— A cock-
fight will take place on Sunday, the 17th inst., at the well-known
house of the subscriber. As the entire proceeds are for the benefit of
the Fire Company, a full attendance is respectfully solicited.

Adam Israng,
Corner of Josephine and Telaupitolas Streets, Lafayette."
[N.O. Pic. of Sunday, Dec. 17.

"Turkey Shooting.—This day, Dec. 17, from 10 o'clock, A.M.,
until 6 o'clock, P.M., and the following Sundays, at M'Donoughville,
opposite the Second Municipality Ferry."

[From the same paper.

The next is an advertisement from the New Orleans Bee, an equally
popular paper.

"A Bull Fight, between a ferocious bull and a number of dogs, will
take place on Sunday next, at 4¼ o'clock P.M., on the other side of
the river, at Algiers, opposite Canal Street. After the bull fight, a
fight will take place between a bear and some dogs. The whole to
conclude by a combat between an ass and several dogs.

"Amateurs bringing dogs to participate in the fight will be
admitted gratis. Admittance—Boxes, 50 cts.; Pit, 30 cts. The
spectacle will be repeated every Sunday, weather permitting.

Pepe Llulla.

Now these are not strange advertisements to be found in a Southern journal. They only show what Slavery has been doing there to contaminate the morals of the people. Such advertisements can be found in numbers of the public journals that are published in the Slave-holding States of this Union. You would not find such an advertisement in a Boston or a Salem paper. Scarcely a paper in New England would admit such an advertisement; and why? Because you are not so closely connected with Slavery; you are not so much under its blighting influence as are the Slave-owners in the Slave-holding States of the Union.

I have another advertisement, taken from a Charleston paper, advertising the property of a deceased Doctor of Divinity, probably one of the most popular men of his denomination that ever resided in the United States of America. In that advertisement it says, that among the property are "twenty-seven Negroes, two mules, one horse, and an old wagon." That is the property of a Slave-holding Doctor of Divinity!*

I have another advertisement before me, taken from an Alabama paper, in which eight Slaves are advertised to be sold for the benefit of an Old School Theological Seminary for the purpose of making ministers. I have another, where ten Slaves are advertised to be sold for the benefit of Christ Church Parish. I have another, where four Slaves are advertised to be sold for the benefit of the Missionary cause,—a very benevolent cause indeed. I might go on and present to you advertisement after advertisement representing the system of American Slavery, and its contaminating influence upon the morals of the people. I have an account, very recent, that a Slave-trader,— one of the meanest and most degrading positions in which a man can be found upon God's footstool,—buying and selling the bodies and souls of his fellow-countrymen, has joined the church, and was, probably, hopefully converted. It is only an evidence that when Wickedness, with a purse of gold, knocks at the door of the Church, she seldom, if ever, is refused admission.

This is not the case here; for, some forty years since, the Church was found repudiating Slavery; she was found condemning Slavery as

---

*Dr. Furman, of South Carolina.

man-stealing, and a sin of the deepest dye. The Methodists, Presbyterians, and other denominations, and some of the first men in the country, bore their testimony against it. But Slavery has gone into all the ramifications of society; it has taken root in almost every part of society, and now Slavery is popular. Slavery has become popular, because it has power.

Speak of the blighting influence of Slavery upon the morals of the people? Go into the Slaveholding States, and there you can see the master going into the church, on the Sabbath, with his Slave following him into the church, and waiting upon him,—both belonging to the same church. And the day following, the master puts his Slave upon the auction-stand, and sells him to the highest bidder. The Church does not condemn him; the law does not condemn him; public sentiment does not condemn him; but the Slaveholder walks through the community as much respected after he has sold a brother belonging to the same church with himself, as if he had not committed an offence against God.

Go into the Slaveholding States, and to-morrow you may see families of Slaves driven to the auction-stand, to be sold to the highest bidder; the husband to be sold in presence of the wife, the wife in presence of the husband, and the children in presence of them both. All this is done under the sanction of law and order; all is done under the sanction of public sentiment, whether that public sentiment be found in Church or in State.

Leaving the Slaveholding States, let me ask what is the influence that Slavery has over the minds of the Northern people? What is its contaminating influence over the great mass of the people of the North? It must have an influence, either good or bad. People of the North, being connected with the Slaveholding States, must necessarily become contaminated. Look all around, and you see benevolent associations formed for the purpose of carrying out the principles of Christianity; but what have they been doing for Humanity? What have they ever done for the slave?

First, we see the great American Bible Society. It is sending bibles all over the world for the purpose of converting the heathen. Its agents are to be found in almost every country and climate. Yet three millions of Slaves have never received a single bible from the

American Bible Society. A few years since, the American Anti-Slavery Society offered to the American Bible Society a donation of $5,000 if they would send bibles to the Slaves, or make an effort to do it, and the American Bible Society refused even to *attempt* to send the bible to the Slaves!

A Bible Society, auxiliary to the American Bible Society, held a meeting a short time since, at Cincinnati, in the State of Ohio. One of its members brought forward a resolution that the Society should do its best to put the bible into the hands of every poor person in the country. As soon as that was disposed of, another member brought forward a resolution that the Society should do its best to put the bible into the hands of every Slave in the country. That subject was discussed for two days, and at the end of that time they threw the resolution under the table, virtually resolving that they would not make an attempt to send bibles to the Slaves.

Leaving the American Bible Society, the next is the American Tract Society. What have you to say against the American Tract Society? you may ask. I have nothing to say against any association that is formed for a benevolent purpose, if it will only carry out the purpose for which it was formed. Has the American Tract Society ever published a single line against the sin of Slaveholding? You have all, probably, read tracts treating against licentiousness, against intemperance, against gambling, against Sabbath-breaking, against dancing, against almost every sin that you can think of; but not a single syllable has ever been published by the American Tract Society against the sin of Slaveholding. Only a short time since they offered a reward of $500 for the best treatise against the sin of dancing. A gentleman wrote the treatise, they awarded him the $500, and the tract is now in the course of publication, if it is not already published. Go into a nice room, with fine music, and good company, and they will publish a tract against your dancing; while three millions are dancing every day at the end of the master's cowhide, and they cannot notice it! Oh, no; it is too small fry for them! They cannot touch that, but they can spend their money in publishing tracts against your dancing here at the North, while the Slave at the South may dance until he dances into his grave, and they care nothing about him.

A friend of mine, residing at Amsterdam, N. Y., who had been
accustomed every year to make a donation to the American Tract

A friend of mine, residing at Amsterdam, N. Y., who had been
accustomed every year to make a donation to the American Tract
and Bible Societies, some two years since said to the Agent when he
was called upon, "I will not give you anything now, but tell the
Board at New York that if they will publish a tract against the sin of
Slaveholding, they may draw on me for $50." The individual's name
is Ellis Clisby, a member of the Presbyterian church, and a more
reputable individual than he cannot be found. The next year when
the Agent called upon him, he asked where was the tract. Said the
Agent, "I laid it before the Committee and they said they dared not
publish it. If they published it their Southern contributions would be
cut off." So they were willing to sacrifice the right, the interest, and
the welfare of the Slave for the "almighty dollar." They were ready
to sacrifice humanity for the sake of receiving funds from the South.
Has not Slavery an influence over the morals of the North?

I have before me an advertisement where some Slaves are
advertised to be sold at the South for the benefit of merchants in the
city of New York, and I will read it to you. It is taken from the
Alabama Beacon.

"Public Sale of Negroes.—By virtue of a deed of trust made to me
by Charles Whelan, for the benefit of J. W. & R. Leavitt, and of
Lewis B. Brown, all of the city of New York, which deed is on record
in Greene County, I shall sell at public auction, for cash, on Main
Street, in the town of Greensborough, on Saturday, the 22d day of
December next, a Negro Woman, about 30 years old, and her child,
eleven months old; a Negro Girl about 10 years old, and a Negro Girl
about 8 years old.

Wm. Trapp, *Trustee.*"

Now if I know anything about the history of this country, the 22d
day of December is the anniversary of the landing of the Pilgrims; the
anniversary of the day when those ambassadors, those leaders in
religion, came to the American shore; when they landed within the
encircling arms of Cape Cod and Cape Ann, fleeing from political and

religious tyranny, seeking political and religious freedom in the New World. The anniversary of that day is selected for selling an American mother and her four children for the benefit of New York merchants.

I happen to know something of one of the parties. He is a member of Dr. Spring's church, and it is said that he gives more money to support that church than any other individual. And I should not wonder, when the bones, and muscles, and sinews, and hearts of human beings are put upon the auction-stand and sold for his benefit, if he could give a little to the church. I should not wonder if he could give a little to some institution that might throw a cloak over him, whitewash him, and make him appear reputable in the community. Has not Slavery an influence over the morals of the North, and of the whole community?

Now let us leave the morals of the American people and look at their character. When I speak of the character of the American people, I look at the nation. I place all together, and draw no mark between the people and the government. The government is the people, and the people are the government. You who are here, all who are to be found in New England, and throughout the United States of America, are the persons that make up the great American confederacy; and I ask, what is the influence that Slavery has had upon the character of the American people? But for the blighting influence of Slavery, the United States of America would have a character, would have a reputation, that would outshine the reputation of any other government that is to be found upon God's green earth.

Look at the struggle of the fathers of this country for liberty. What did they struggle for? What did they go upon the battle-field for, in 1776? They went there, it is said, for the purpose of obtaining liberty; for the purpose of instituting a democratic, republican government. What is Democracy? Solon, upon one occasion, while speaking to the Athenians said, "A democratic government is a government where an injury done to the least of its citizens is regarded as an insult and an injury to the whole commonwealth." That was the opinion of an old law-maker and statesman upon the subject of Democracy. But what says an American statesman? A South Carolina governor says that Slavery is the corner-stone of our

Republic. Another eminent American states...
hundred years have sanctioned and sanctified A...
that is property which the law declares to be pr...
we believe? One that is reared in republican Ame...
brought up in the lap of aristocracy? Every one...
democracy is nothing more or less than genuine fre......... liberty,
protecting every individual in the community.

I might carry the audience back to the time when your fathers
were struggling for liberty in 1776. When they went forth upon the
battle-field and laid down their bones, and moistened the soil with
their blood, that their children might enjoy liberty. What was it for?
Because a three-penny tax upon tea, a tax upon paper, or something
else had been imposed upon them. We are not talking against such
taxes upon the Slave. The Slave has no tea; he has no paper; he has
not even himself; he has nothing at all.

When we examine the influence of Slavery upon the character of
the American people, we are led to believe that if the American
Government ever had a character, she has lost it. I know that upon
4th of July, our 4th of July orators talk of Liberty, Democracy, and
Republicanism. They talk of liberty, while three millions of their
own countrymen are groaning in abject Slavery. This is called the
"land of the free, and the home of the brave;" it is called the
"Asylum of the oppressed;" and some have been foolish enough to
call it the "Cradle of Liberty." If it is the "cradle of liberty," they
have rocked the child to death. It is dead long since, and yet we talk
about democracy and republicanism, while one-sixth of our countrymen are clanking their chains upon the very soil which our fathers
moistened with their blood. They have such scenes even upon the
holy Sabbath, and the American people are perfectly dead upon the
subject. The cries, and shrieks, and groans of the Slave do not wake
them.

It is deplorable to look at the character of the American people,
the character that has been given to them by the institution of
Slavery. The profession of the American people is far above the
profession of the people of any other country. Here the people
profess to carry out the principles of Christianity. The American
people are a sympathising people. They not only profess, but appear
to be a sympathizing people to the inhabitants of the whole world.

sympathise with everything else but the American Slave. When the Greeks were struggling for liberty, meetings were held to express sympathy. Now they are sympathising with the poor down-trodden serfs of Ireland, and are sending their sympathy across the ocean to them.

But what will the poeple of the Old World think? Will they not look upon the American people as hypocrites? Do they not look upon your professed sympathy as nothing more than hypocrisy? You may hold your meetings and send your words across the ocean; you may ask Nicholas of Russia to take the chains from his poor down-trodden serfs, but they look upon it all as nothing but hypocrisy. Look at our twenty thousand fugitive Slaves, running from under the stars and stripes, and taking refuge in the Canadas; *twenty thousand,* some leaving their wives, some their husbands, some leaving their children, some their brothers, and some their sisters,—fleeing to take refuge in the Canadas. Wherever the stars and stripes are seen flying in the United States of America, they point him out as a Slave.

If I wish to stand up and say, "I am a man," I must leave the land that gave me birth. If I wish to ask protection as a man, I must leave the American stars and stripes. Wherever the stars and stripes are seen flying upon American soil, I can receive no protection; I am a Slave, a chattel, a thing. I see your liberty-poles around in your cities. If to-morrow morning you are hoisting the stars and stripes upon one of your liberty-poles, and I should see the man following me who claims my body and soul as his property, I might climb to the very top of your liberty-pole, I might cut the cord that held your stars and stripes and bind myself with it as closely as I could to your liberty-pole, I might talk of law and the Constitution, but nothing could save me unless there be public sentiment enough in Salem. I could not appeal to law or the Constitution; I could only appeal to public sentiment; and if public sentiment would not protect me, I must be carried back to the plantations of the South, there to be lacerated, there to drag the chains that I left upon the Southern soil a few years since.

This is deplorable; and yet the American Slave *can* find a spot where he may be a man;—but it is not under the American flag. Fellow citizens, I am the last to eulogise any country where they oppress the poor. I have nothing to say in behalf of England or any other country, any further than as they extend protection to mankind. I say that I honor England for protecting the black man. I honor every country that shall receive the American Slave, that shall protect him, and that shall recognise him as a man.

I know that the United States will not do it; but I ask you to look at the efforts of other countries. Even the Bey of Tunis, a few years since, has decreed that there shall not be a Slave in his dominions; and we see that the subject of liberty is being discussed throughout the world. People are looking at it; they are examining it; and it seems as though every country, and every people, and every goverment were doing something, excepting the United States. But Christian, democratic, republican America is doing nothing at all. It seems as though she would be the last. It seems as though she was determined to be the last to knock the chain from the limbs of the Slave. Shall the American people be behind the people of the Old World? Shall they be behind those who are represented as almost living in the dark ages?

> "Shall every flap of England's flag
> Proclaim that all around are free,
> From farthest Ind to each blue crag
> That beetles o'er the western sea?
> And shall we scoff at Europe's kings,
> When Freedom's fire is dimmed with us;
> And round our country's altar clings
> The damning shade of Slavery's curse?"

Shall we, I ask, shall the American people be the last? I am here, not for the purpose of condemning the character of the American people, but for the purpose of trying to protect or vindicate their character. I would to God that there was some feature that I could vindicate. There is no liberty here for me; there is no liberty for those with whom I am associated; there is no liberty for the American Slave; and yet we hear a great deal about liberty! How do the people of the Old World regard the American people? Only a short time since, an American gentleman, in travelling through Germany, passed the window of a bookstore where he saw a number of pictures. One of them was a cut representing an American Slave on his knees, with chains upon his limbs. Over him stood a white man, with a long whip; and underneath was written, "the latest specimen of American democracy." I ask my audience, who placed that in the hands of those that drew it? I was the people of the United States. Slavery, as it is to be found in this country, has given the serfs of the Old World an opportunity of branding the American people as the most tyrannical people upon God's footstool.

Only a short time since an American man-of-war was anchored in the bay opposite Liverpool. The English came down by the hundreds and thousands. The stars and stripes were flying; and there stood those poor persons that had never seen an American man-of-war, but had heard a great deal of American democracy. Some were eulogising the American people; some were calling it the "land of the free and the home of the brave." And while they stood there, one of their number rose up, and pointing his fingers to the American flag, said:

> "United States, your banner wears
> Two emblems,—one of fame;
> Alas, the other that it bears,
> Reminds us of your shame.
> The white man's liberty entyped,
> Stands blazoned by your stars;
> But what's the meaning of your stripes?
> They mean your Negro-scars."

What put that in the mouth of that individual? It was the system of American Slavery; it was the action of the American people; the inconsistency of the American people; their profession of liberty, and their practice in opposition to their profession.

I find that the time admonishes me that I am going on too far; but when I get upon this subject, and find myself surrounded by those who are willing to listen, and who seem to sympathise with my down-trodden countrymen, I feel that I have a great duty to discharge. Now matter what the people may say upon this subject; no matter what they may say against the great Anti-Slavery movement of this country; I believe it is the Anti-Slavery movement that is calculated to redeem the character of the American people. Much as I have said against the character of the American people this evening, I believe that it is the Anti-Slavery movement of this country that is to redeem its character. Nothing can redeem it but the principles that are advocated by the friends of the Slave in this country.

I look upon this as one of the highest and noblest movements of the age. William Lloyd Garrison, a few years since, planted the tree of Liberty, and that tree has taken root in all branches of Government. That tree was not planted for a day, a week, a month, or a year; but to stand till the last chain should fall from the limbs of the last Slave in the United States of America, and in the world. It is a tree that will stand. Yes, it was planted of the very best plant that could be found among the great plants in the world.

> "Our plant is of the cedar,
> That knoweth not decay;
> Its growth shall bless the mountains,
> Till mountains pass away;
> Its top shall greet the sunshine,
> Its leaves shall drink the rain,
> While on its lower branches
> The Slave shall hang his chain."

Yes, it is a plant that will stand. The living tree shall grow up and shall not only liberate the Slave in this country, but shall redeem the character of the American people.

The efforts of the American people not only to keep the Slaves in Slavery, but to add new territory, and to spread the institution of Slavery all over Christendom,—their high professions and their inconsistency, have done more to sadden the hearts of the reformers in the Old World than anything else that could have been thought of. The reformers and lovers of liberty in the Old World look to the American Government, look to the lovers of liberty in America, to aid them in knocking the chains from their own limbs in Europe, to aid them in elevating themselves; but instead of their receiving cooperation from the Government of the United States, instead of their being cheered on by the people of the United States, the people and the Government have done all that they could to oppose liberty, to oppose democracy, and to oppose reform.

Go to the capital of our country, the city of Washington; the capital of the freest government upon the face of the world. Only a few days since, an American mother and her daughter were sold upon the auction-block in that city, and the money was put into the Treasury of the United States of America. Go there and you can scarcely stand an hour but you will see caufles of Slaves driven past the Capitol, and likely as not you will see the foremost one with the stars and stripes in his hand; and yet the American Legislators, the people of the North and of the South, the "assembled wisdom" of the nation, look on and see such things and hold their peace; they say not a single word against such oppression, or in favor of liberty.

In conclusion let me say, that the character of the American people and the influence of Slavery upon that character have been blighting and withering the efforts of all those that favor liberty, reform, and progression. But it has not quite accomplished it. There are those who are willing to stand by the Slave. I look upon the great Anti-Slavery platform as one upon which those who stand, occupy the same position,—I would say, a higher position, than those who put forth their Declaration in 1776, in behalf of American liberty. Yes, the American Abolitionists now occupy a higher and holier position than those who carried on the American Revolution. They do not want that that husband should be any longer sold from his wife. They want that the husband should have a right to protect his wife; that the brother should have a right to protect his sister. They are tired and sick at heart in seeing human beings placed upon the auction-block and sold to the highest bidder. They want that man should be protected. They want that a stop should be put to this system of iniquity and bloodshed; and they are laboring for its overthrow.

I would that every one here could go into the Slave-States, could go where I have been, and see the workings of Slavery upon the Slave. When I get to talking upon this subject I am carried back to the day when I saw a dear mother chained and carried off in a Southern steamboat to supply the cotton, sugar, or rice plantations of the South. I am carried back to the day when a dear sister was sold and carried off in my presence. I stood and looked at her. I could not protect her. I could not offer to protect her. I was a Slave, and the only testimony that I could give her that I sympathised with her, was to allow the tears to flow freely down my cheeks; and the tears flowing freely down her cheeks told me that my affection was reciprocated. I am carried back to the day when I saw three dear brothers sold, and carried off.

When I speak of Slavery I am carried back to the time when I saw, day after day, my own fellow-country men placed upon the auction-stand; when I saw the bodies, and sinews, and hearts, and the souls of men sold to the highest bidder. I have with me an account of a Slave recently sold upon the auction-stand. The auctioneer could only get a bid of $400, but as he was about to knock her off, the owner of the Slave made his way through those that surrounded him and whispered to the auctioneer. As soon as the owner left, the auctioneer said, "I have failed to tell you all the good qualities of this Slave. I have told you that she was strong, healthy, and hearty, and now I have the pleasure to announce to you that she is very pious. She has got religion." And although, before that, he could only get $400, as soon as they found that she had got religion they commenced bidding upon her, and the bidding went up to $700. The writer says that her body and mind were sold for $400, and her religion was sold for $300. My friends, I am aware that there are people at the North who would sell their religion for a $5 bill, and make money on it; and that those who purchased it would get very much cheated in the end. But the piety of the Slave differs from the piety of the people in the nominally free States. The piety of the Slave is to be a good servant.

This is a subject in which I ask your cooperation. I hope that every individual here will take hold and help carry on the Anti-Slavery movement. We are not those who would ask the men to help us and leave the women at home. We want all to help us. A million of women are in Slavery, and as long as a single woman is in Slavery, every woman in the community should raise her voice against that sin, that crying evil that is degrading her sex. I look to the rising generation. I expect that the rising generation will liberate the Slave. I do not look to the older ones. I have sometimes thought that the sooner we got rid of the older ones the better it would be. The older ones have got their old prejudices, and their old associations, and they cling to them, and seem not to look at the Slave or to care anything about him.

Now, fellow-citizens, when you shall return home, and be scattered around your several firesides, and when you have an opportunity to make a remark about what I have said here this evening, all I ask of you is to give the cause, justice; to give what I have said, justice. Give it a fair investigation. If you have not liked my grammar, recollect that I was born and brought up under an institution, where, if an individual was found teaching me, he would have been sent to the State's Prison. Recollect that I was brought up where I had not the privilege of education. Recollect that you have come here to-night to hear a Slave, and not a man, according to the laws of the land; and if the Slave has failed to interest you, charge it not to the race, charge it not to the colored people, but charge it to the blighting influences of Slavery,—that institution that has made me property, and that is making property of three millions of my countrymen at the present day. Charge it upon that institution that is annihilating the minds of three millions of my countrymen. Charge it upon that institution, whether found in the political arena or in the American churches. Charge it upon that institution, cherished by the American people, and looked upon as the essence of Democracy,—upon *American Slavery*.

DATE DUE

DEC 5 '78			
DEC 6 '78			
DE 14 '77			
DE 4 '79			
DE 14 '79			
NO 17 '81			
OC 20 '80			
			PRINTED IN U.S.A.
GAYLORD			